DESSERT CLUB

How to Find and Taste Sensational Global Sweets

DESSERT CLUB

BY DIANE BORSATO

ILLUSTRATIONS BY KELSEY OSEID

CHRONICLE BOOKS
SAN FRANCISCO

Library of Congress Cataloging-in-Publication Data
Names: Borsato, Diane author | Oseid, Kelsey illustrator
Title: Dessert club : how to find and taste sensational global sweets / by Diane Borsato ; illustrations Kelsey Oseid.
Description: San Francisco : Chronicle Books, [2026] | Includes bibliographical references.
Identifiers: LCCN 2026014152 | ISBN 9781797234779 hardcover
Subjects: LCSH: Desserts | Baking | LCGFT: Cookbooks
Classification: LCC TX773 .B6425 2026 | DDC 641.86—dc23/eng/20260401
LC record available at https://lccn.loc.gov/2026014152

Manufactured in China.

FSC www.fsc.org MIX Paper | Supporting responsible forestry FSC™ C008047

Design by Zoë Carr.
Cover design by Kayla Ferriera.
Typeset in Arquitecta, Quicksand, Meltow San, Savate,
Baze, Salvaje Display, Froople, and Swear Display.

10 9 8 7 6 5 4 3 2 1

Chronicle Books is represented in the UK and Europe by Abrams & Chronicle Books, 22 Ely Place, London EC1N 6TE, abramsandchronicle.co.uk, and Média-Participations, 57 rue Gaston Tessier, 75166 Paris CEDEX 19, media-participations.com.

Chronicle Books LLC
680 Second Street
San Francisco, California 94107
chroniclebooks.com

CONTENTS

INTRODUCTION: HOW TO EAT DESSERT 10

DESSERTS 17

Almond Cake & Pistachio Cake 18

Babka 22

Baked Alaska 25

Biscoff Cheesecake 30

Booza & Ice Cream Sandwich 34

Bubble Tea 38

Bubble Waffle Hotdog & Bacon Donut 48

Canelé 52

Cannoli 55

Charcoal Ice Cream 59

Chocolate Shot & Lava Cake 63

Coconut Jellies & Sweet Corn, Tapioca, and Coconut Pudding 68

Crepe Cake 72
Cupcake with Buttercream 75
Éclair & Cream Puff 78
Fat Bomb 83
Fruit Sando 86
Gulab Jamun 89
Halo-Halo 93
Ispahan 97
Kakigori & Bingsu 100
Kashmiri Chai 104
Kunafa & Mahalabiyeh 107
Lemon Lavender Shortbread 113
Mango Pomelo Sago 116
Maple Syrup Pie 120
Matcha Parfait & Flower Parfait 124
Medovik 130
Mille-Feuilles 134

Mochi Donuts 138
Mont Blanc 141
Mooncake 145
Pavlova & Lamingtons 148
Pineapple Chamoyada 154
Plant-Based Cheesecake 157
Rainbow Cake 160
Raindrop Cake & Anmitsu 164
Rhubarb Pudding 168
Royal Falooda 171
Soufflé Pancakes 174
Sticky Toffee Pudding 177
Strawberry Shortcake 180
Taiyaki 184
Tanghulu 188
Tiramisu & Banana Pudding 192
Tres Leches Cake 196

Trompe l'Oeil Dessert & Entremet 199

Vanilla Custard Tart & Fruit Custard Tart 205

Wagashi 210

War Cake 215

Wild Blueberry Pie 218

Zoolbia & Gaz 222

THE DESSERT CLUB LIFE LIST 226

ACKNOWLEDGMENTS 251

ENDNOTES 254

ABOUT THE CREATORS 256

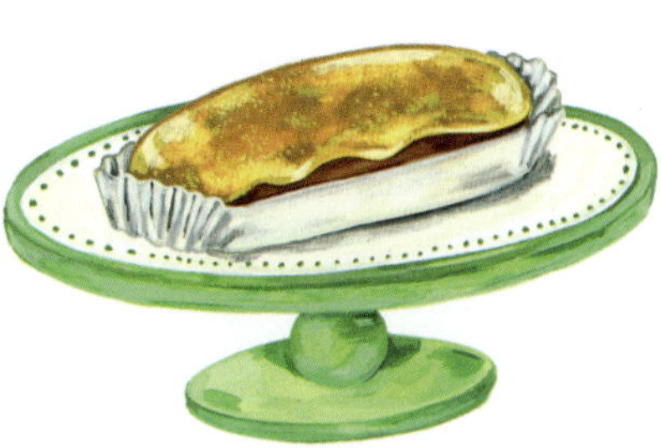

INTRODUCTION:

HOW TO EAT DESSERT

Considering the lines of enthusiastic patrons stretching down the block outside of bakeries, chocolatiers, and fine pastry shops, I know I'm not alone in my love for desserts. I live in Toronto, a cosmopolitan metropolis where more than a hundred languages are spoken and half of our population was born in another part of the world. Ours is a city of vibrant, diverse neighborhoods, so I can easily find crunchy Cannoli in Little Italy, buttery rum cake in Little Jamaica, and a hot, fish-shaped, custard-filled waffle, or Taiyaki, in Koreatown, all within walking distance from my home. After just a short bus ride to the east, I can eat a fresh baklava in the Greek neighborhood and wash it down with a pink Kashmiri Chai sprinkled with green pistachios in Little India. There is a Little Manila community in the north where I can meet a friend for Halo-Halo, and if we aren't satisfied yet, we will not be far from enclaves of Venezuelan, Colombian, and Mexican restaurants that serve buñuelos and Tres Leches Cake in a deep pool of milky sauce. To add to this splendor, the greater Toronto area has at least *six* Chinatowns where I can find a deep cooling bowl of Mango Pomelo Sago, bright purple potato ice cream, and many more of the most inventive, delicious treats.

I hope you can use this book as a field guide to popular desserts, even if your field—by which I mean your own big city or one you happen to be visiting—is in a different part of the globe than my own. So many of the colorful desserts in this book can be found in any populous international city near you, because along with the people from around the world who settle there come the most beloved ingredients and gastronomic traditions, mixing and multiplying into a sugar-fueled phantasmagoria of possibilities.

This book is about the cakes, meringues, puddings, donuts, Bundts, pies, ice creams, and more that I have found at bakeries and sweet shops over the last few years. Not only has the "research" been so fun (eating a lot of desserts, and then jogging while listening to podcasts about chocolate), but I am also thankful that lingering over these experiences and sharing my notes and stories with you have given me the pleasure of enjoying them all over again.

I should confess that in my selections, I'm limited by a few logistical factors. These include the specific places I have lived and visited (and those I haven't), along with my perspective as an Italian Canadian tea lover living in Toronto. And not only is this a short book but I definitely have my biases. I'm especially partial to anything flavored with strawberry, matcha, vanilla, or pistachio; swimming with tapioca pearls; enveloped in a shattering crust; or buried in a pool of custard. When I make my recommendations, I don't know what desserts you already know and love, or where you have been, or where you will begin. I hope you might forgive my overexplaining (or even misunderstanding) the details of dishes that are unusual and thrilling to me—like Korean Bingsu in the summertime, Gulab Jamun for Eid, or a spiraling Persian Zoolbia served under a chandelier—but that may be common and familiar to you.

No matter what dessert experience you have, I hope you will find enough inspiration and insight in this guide to taste a new slice, a pouf, an orb, a stack, a puddle, or a gorgeous tumbling heap of something sweet at your own café table, maybe even under a chandelier. I hope you will feel encouraged to savor a dessert wherever you are: mingling among crowds on a busy street, alone in the park, or even on the subway if you can't wait to dig in.

I also want this book to alert you to the trendiest new pancakes, the jet-black ice cream everyone is posing with, and some essential vocabulary for ordering a Bubble Tea. You are invited to taste a world of flavors in a spectrum of colors, to revel in the quirky delights of Bacon Donuts, spicy pineapples, syrupy noodles, and Éclairs sprinkled with gold. Explore the curiosities of molecular gastronomy (hopefully without having to order an expensive dinner first) in elegant odes to lemons and in wobbling spheres of water gelatinized to look like glass. Learn about Crepe Cakes, Fat Bombs, and whipped cream sandwiches. Imagine Coconut Jellies delivered by bicycle, a cup of molten chocolate, and a laundry basket full of jackfruit and flan. If you trust me enough to follow this guide, you will discover nothing less than drinks you can chew, clouds you can eat, and fruit that tastes like diamonds. I hope that this book makes the case once and for all that dessert is an everyday delight.

In this volume, you will also meet some dignified makers and rapturous lovers of dessert. Appreciate and support them. These are the bakers and chocolatiers and tireless Baked Alaska makers, as well as the chestnut puree extruders, the ice shavers, and the maple tree tappers in the snow. You will learn about the roles of queens and emperors and divas, mothers and grandmothers and celebrity chefs, hungry teenagers, and at least one ballerina tiptoeing across the stage in the teeniest steps en pointe. Together, the people who craft and enjoy dessert infuse it with much meaning, from feats of aesthetic refinement to assertions of dignity during wartime rationing.

Desserts are made and shared to bring joy and deepen belonging, to express identity and summon pride. We gather around desserts to remember traditions and, sometimes, to invent radical new ones. We celebrate the land and the seasons and share dessert to mark our most important rituals together in the passing of our lives. Every dessert I write about here is a small celebration of these gifts and wonders.

The desserts I have included in *Dessert Club* are not too difficult to find and are affordable for most of us. In a world rife with so much disconnection and misunderstanding, each one represents a brief but insistent moment of connection and happiness. In his own collection of food memories, *A Thousand Feasts*, the chef and food writer Nigel Slater describes what it means to revel in a bite of honeyed mango or a sip of roasted tea: "I have no interest in living in a rose-tinted bubble, but if I have learned one thing, it is not only to concentrate on the 'positive stuff,' but to cherish it. I will admit to seeking it out, to looking up instead of down, to being curious and to hold on, as tightly as I can, to the 'good things,' however small."[1]

Dessert is small, but necessary. It tastes better because it has been made for us with care; because it's the last day of school in a heat wave; because we are layering a sundae and laughing with an old friend; or because we are enjoying it while listening to the sounds of Punjabi hip-hop music coming from a car driving by. Sometimes we savor sweet things to feel our own bodily presence on Earth, to revel in beauty and imagination, to ease our sorrows, or to submit ourselves to love.

Even if it takes a lifetime, I invite you to find and experience all the desserts in this book. Taste the ones you already adore and try new things you learn about here. Then go on to enjoy more delicious desserts from around the world that you, or I, haven't even dreamed of yet.

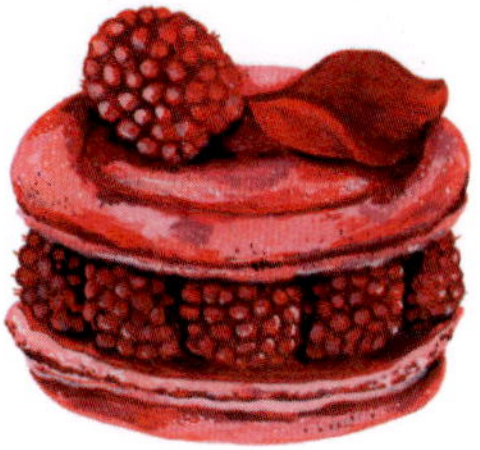

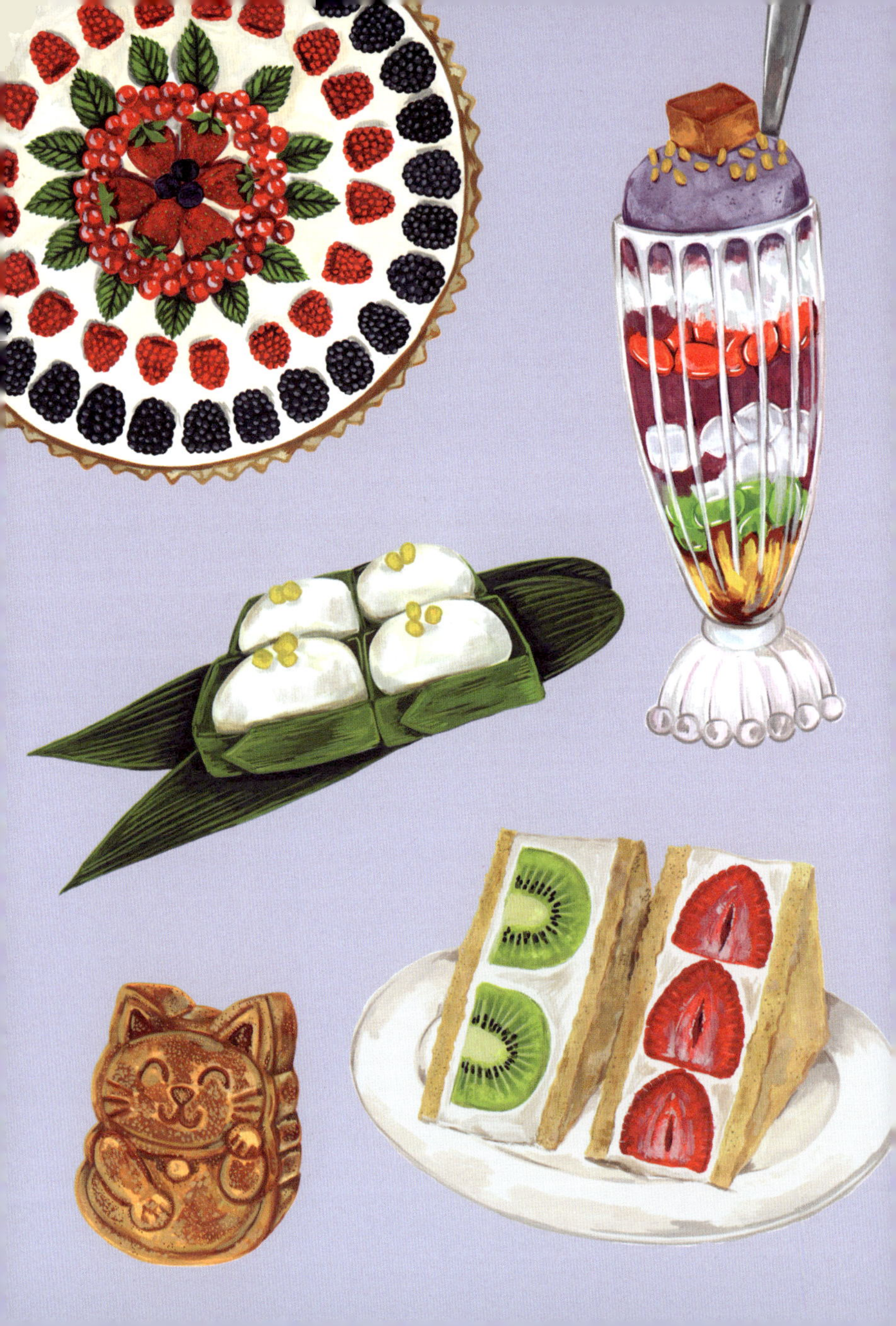

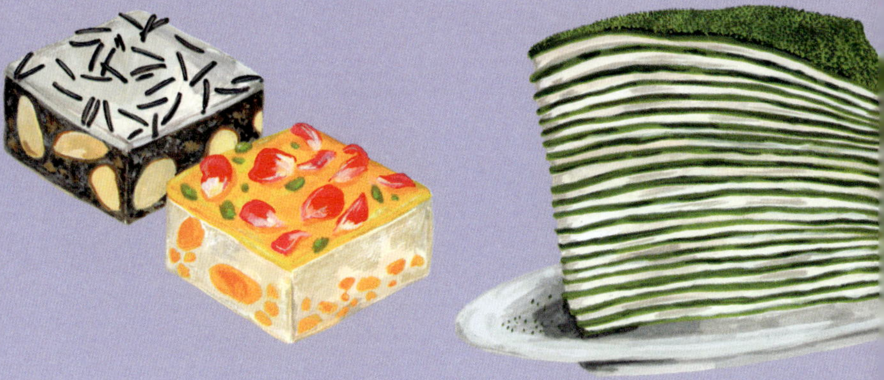

DESSERTS

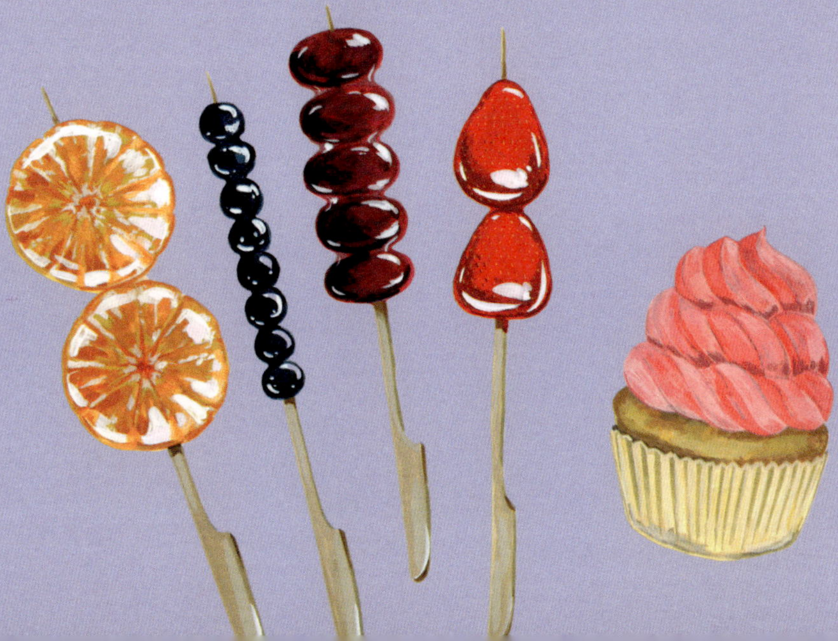

Almond Cake & Pistachio Cake

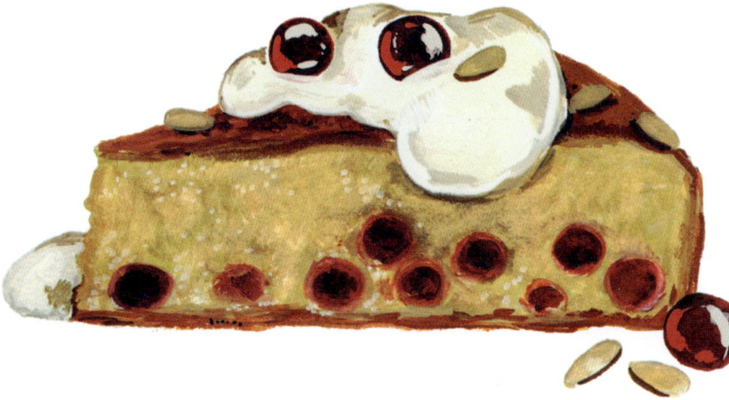

Almond Cake with Sour Cherries and Yogurt Cream

Order the nut cake! Based on decades of experience, this is one of the most reliable shortcuts in the face of complex dessert decisions, and among my favorite rules for living. Some of the finest cakes I've ever eaten have been almond, pistachio, walnut, hazelnut, or chestnut cakes. It's easy for anyone to love the nourishing kick of substance, the perfume, and the most luxurious of nutty fats. It's possible that as a Northern Italian, I'm genetically predisposed to adoring the bittersweet-ness and crunch of this regional bounty because my ancestors have included them in almost everything celebratory, special, and delicious for centuries.

My family loves Italian chocolate sponge cakes, chunky with embedded nuts, along with a cup of espresso in winter. I tend toward the plainer variations, the cakes that center the distinctive aromatic charms of just one nut at a time. These are made with ground nut meal, only minimally lightened with wheat flour, if it is used at all. They are the ones that you see in the display case of a good café, practically translucent with oils and glowing with ambient windowlight. Trust me and order that cake.

The best of all the nut cakes I've tasted have come after a restaurant meal, arriving at the table very fresh, soft, and warm. I tasted an Almond Cake with soft, melting sour cherries at a swanky Middle Eastern restaurant that made me forget everything else I ate there, or that I ate at all, for days. The toasty, woody flavor of Almond Cake is brightened by tart red fruit and, in this case, a dollop of refreshing yogurt cream. If you can find a dessert like this, with every satisfying element in contrast and balance, it will carry you away with contentedness.

I am also thrilled by the rich and dense kinds of Pistachio Cake that—despite how expensive pistachios are—are increasingly available in coffee shops and on fashionable restaurant dessert menus. These are the luxurious green cakes that drench your napkins with oil, and might even moisturize your hands! Try to find a Pistachio Cake made with rosewater, rose petals, citrus

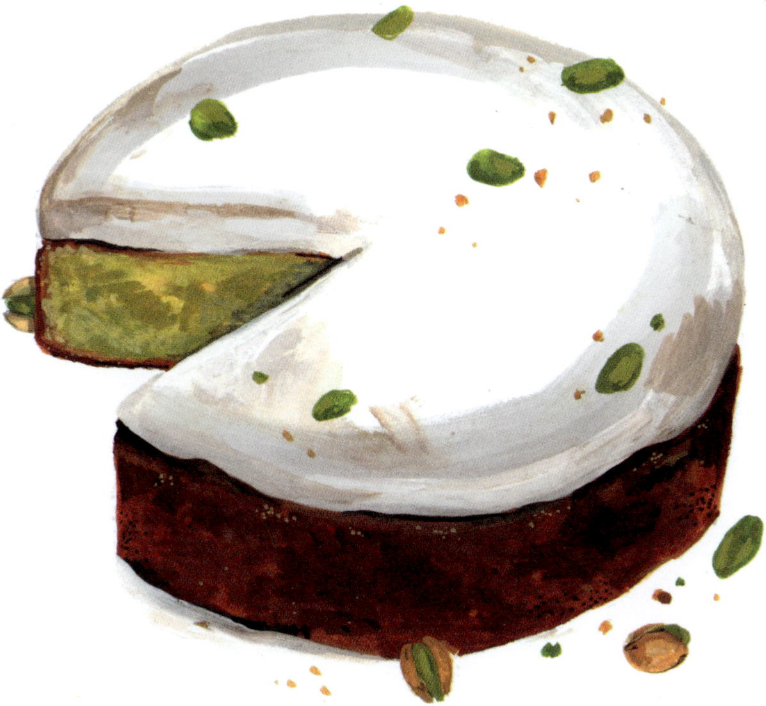

Pistachio Cake with Rosewater

zests, or all three—or anything else, because (as the Italians, who even put them on pizza, know) pistachios go with everything. Lift a glass with your buttery fingerprints all over it, and express your gratitude for the very fine gifts of trees.

BABKA

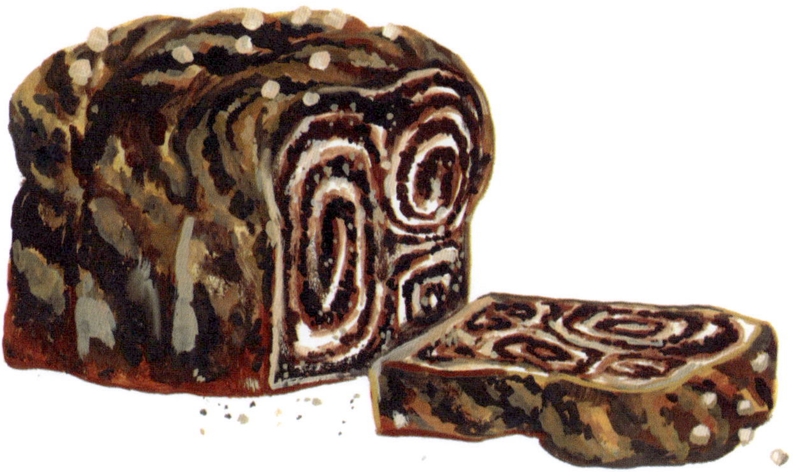

Chocolate Babka

I was not surprised to discover that the word *babka* is probably a variation of an Eastern European word for "grandmother." The association is strong with the Russian word *babushka*, meaning old woman or grandmother; *bubba*, *bubbie*, or *bobe*, each endearing terms in Yiddish for "grandmother"; and *baba* in Polish and Serbian. These are all related words for the same woman, who, if you are lucky, flattens out great, wide slabs of sweetened bread dough and sprinkles them with cinnamon, honey, or chocolate. She rolls the slabs into heavy ropes, twists and braids them again and again, and leaves the cake to rise. While you watch it form buttery bulges, stained magma arches, and undulating pastry folds, she might even tell you stories about yourself as a ravenous child.

But don't fret! Without one of these mythical ladies, or with a grandmother who lacks confidence in the presence of a bowl of live yeast, there are other ways to earn your own Babka. This is most often achieved by standing in line for a fresh loaf at the best local Jewish, Polish, or Ukrainian bakery. Finding the long line is a part of this task, so ask around. If you want one of the famously good Babkas in your city, you will need to make a pilgrimage to where they are sold fresh and warm by the dozen, or even by the hundred, to all their loyal devotees.

Go where the fluffy, croissant-like dough is made rich with butter and folded together with chocolate, cinnamon, dried fruit, halvah, citrus, or nuts in a sumptuous, loaf pan-wide plait.

A Babka dries out quickly, so just as soon as you can get your hands on one you should wrap it loosely for storage. Warm it gently before consumption, being careful not to burn the delicate dough, and then eat it right away. (Don't you love an urgency rule like this?) I like to unfold and deconstruct the twisting swirls, enjoyably unmaking the sticky Babka vortices before I put them in my mouth. A Babka is not just a humble family cake. It's an enveloping landscape of memory and love, a topography of deliciousness.

BAKED ALASKA

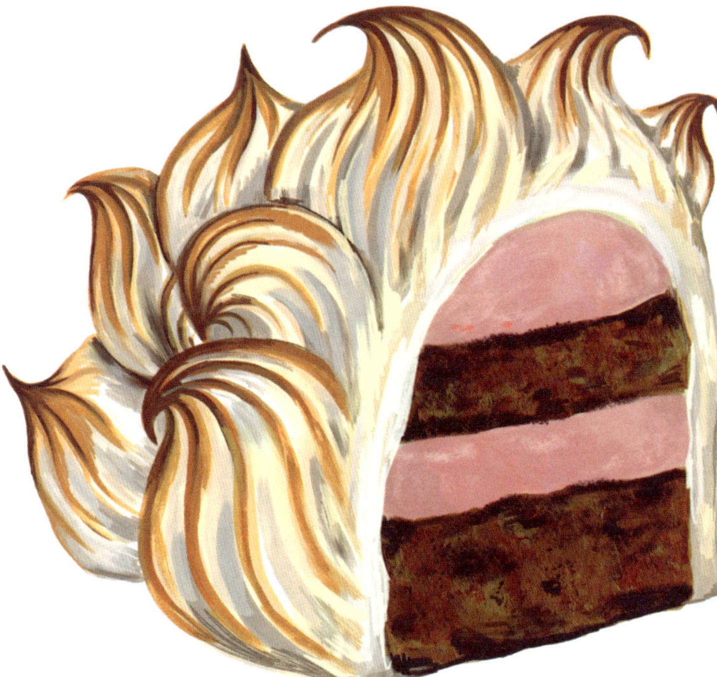

Baked Alaska

I knew I could find a beautiful example of Baked Alaska in New York City. What I didn't realize was that it would be at Gage & Tollner, a Brooklyn restaurant that has been in operation since the 1870s, while sitting on a red velvet banquette surrounded by polished cherry wood, white marble, and silk brocade paneling. Around me, the warm golden lighting was amplified by a dizzying matrix of gleaming brass and shining mirrors, reflecting the splendor in all directions. It was so transporting from the noisy city street outside that I was reminded that the dessert I came to find was part of another era entirely. Like the room, Baked Alaska is a time capsule from America's Gilded Age. I wasn't just dreaming of that era and place for the evening; I could actually taste it.

Baked Alaska was invented in New York in 1867 by a chef tasked with celebrating the purchase of Alaska from the Russian Empire. To embody the union of warm southern states with a new, icy northern one, it was first named "Alaska Florida." Then, as now, the dessert consisted of layers of cake and ice cream, all enrobed in a thick layer of warm, toasty meringue. In the 1970s, when it was really in fashion, housewives were instructed to make it by layering sliced blocks of store-bought Neapolitan ice cream onto a flan base covered with canned fruit, finally topping everything with a thick layer of Italian-style meringue. All the elements were frozen ice-cold and hard together, before the cook had to put it into—and then quickly take it out of—a very hot oven, achieving the impressive signature feature of a Baked Alaska: its warm and burnished meringue in stark contrast to a freezing cold cake-and-ice-cream center.

You might find a 1970s version, more or less like the one I described, in a fine American restaurant. Or maybe it will be a 1980s version, from when chefs started pouring alcohol over the Baked Alaska and setting it ablaze at the table to add even more awe and drama. The contemporary dessert I was lucky to taste in Brooklyn was entirely handmade by the celebrated pastry chef Caroline Schiff, from its chocolate cookie crumb base through the house-made vanilla and Amarena cherry, chocolate, and mint ice creams and all the way up to the highest peak of its silky meringue coat. Described in the menu as being "for two," the whole wispy glacier-like creation that was set in front of my friend Abby and me was nearly a foot high!

In an interview with *Bon Appétit* magazine,[2] Schiff described the work of constructing the Baked Alaska as having her arms—literally—up to her elbows in a sticky ice cream churning machine. The entire process takes her restaurant team a total of three days: mix and churn custard, chill and layer contrasting stripes of ice cream, paddle on the thickest insulating blanket of meringue, and finally torch it all for effect. Only then can it be whisked off, as fast as possible, to lucky diners in a red-velvet banquette—diners like you, I hope, who will need to take a deep breath before plunging your spoon into the elegant dessert mountain, through silky warmth and sweetened cold and all the opulence of both the dessert and the bygone era of careless wealth it represents. Heave it all into your mouth before it topples, as things like this always do, into a dreamy heap.

BISCOFF CHEESECAKE

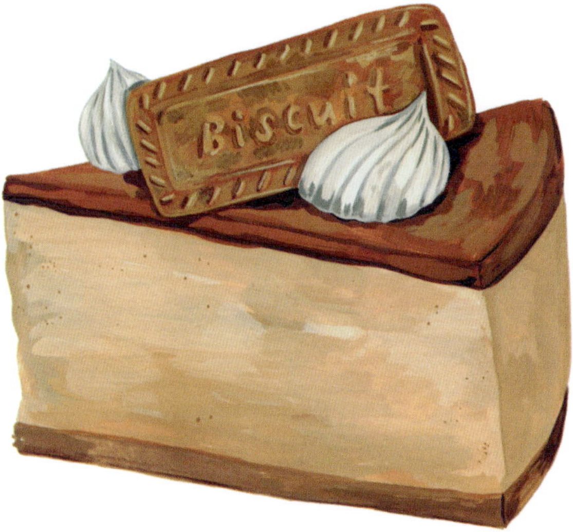

Biscoff Cheesecake

I was treading water in an extra-cold swimming pool and dreaming about a cup of hot tea when my companion, a young Iranian dessert lover, declared Biscoff her favorite flavor, and Biscoff Cheesecake her all-time best-loved dessert. I am embarrassed to have been so ignorant of youthful dessert tastes at the time. "Biscoff?" I asked her, while splashing around. "What is Biscoff?"

After consulting with a critical mass of globalized urban teenagers who love Biscoff Cheesecake and everything else flavored with the ubiquitous cinnamon biscuit, I learned a few things I can finally share. *Biscoff* is a brand name for cookies that are cinnamony, caramelized brown sugar rectangles, a little oily, a little crunchy, and a comfort to dunk in your coffee. Sometimes they are called *Lotus cookies*, after the Belgian parent company that makes them. You have probably eaten a few, offered to you by a kind steward on an airplane, from a tidy red-and-white foil packet. It's one of the rare things handed out on airplanes that tastes fresh and crisp and that, in uncomfortable and perhaps nervous circumstances, brings a little comfort. In fact, on my last flight, I noticed the airline was boasting of having given away sixty million of the biscuits, together weighing "more than 1,687 tons"! It's an impressive load of cookies flying through the air above us, and I like to imagine that legions of people are probably nibbling on them right now up in the clouds.

You might know the cookies—or one of their lookalikes—under a range of brand names. But did you know that there is also a sticky, chewy sandwich spread made with the same flavoring? And that you can find pillowy bags of smashed biscuits for an infinite number of recipes designed to feature them? Because of this, cookie cheesecakes, ice creams, tarts, and puddings have taken over dessert counters and displays, making Biscoff (and the rest) an ultra-popular new global flavor and garnish.

The spicy bite and delicate crunch of these biscuits pair especially well with a plain, light, creamy cheesecake filling, with layers of the chewy spread like a dense, almost gritty caramel. A Biscoff Cheesecake is a treat so rich it could probably replace a meal, warm a shivery body, prompt an enduring sleep, and inspire contented dreams. This is a powerful dessert! I can see why a chilly teenager, treading water like her life depended on it, was fantasizing about it. So, do all your laps in the cold pool, then bring your appetite for this epic indulgence, wherever you can find it.

Booza & Ice Cream Sandwich

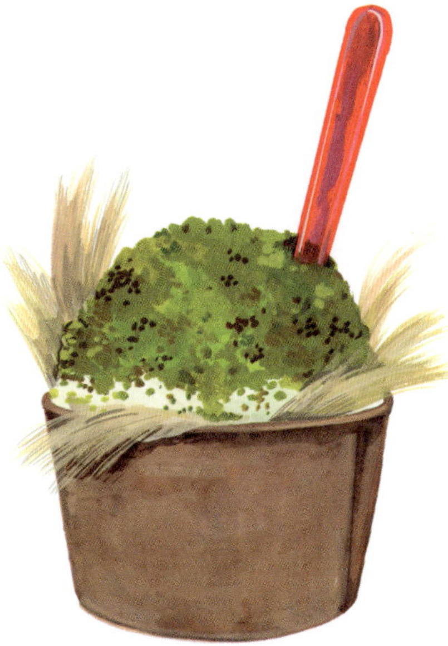

Booza with Pistachios and Ghazl el Banet

Picture a cool and resinous ice cream flavored by an evergreen shrub and made stretchy as wet marshmallows from the powdered starch of an orchid tuber. Dip it into a barrel of chopped pistachios until it is covered all over with a nutty, crunchy green crust. Throw in a wedge of crispy, shredded knafeh pastry, or even some ghazl el banet (a threadlike white cotton candy) to swirl and shimmer all around it like a cirrus cloud. What you will have is an all-dressed-up, gorgeous, and delicious Middle Eastern treat called *Booza*.

While this might be familiar to dessert lovers from Lebanon, Egypt, the UAE, and surrounding environs, you might be surprised to learn that it is more common and easily available than you imagine. Any big city with a significant Middle Eastern community should have purveyors of this extraordinary treat. After all, if you grew up with ice cream like this, would you agree to live anywhere without it? Look for what is sometimes called Lebanese or Arabic ice cream. Choose among various fruity, nutty, and floral flavors—like rose or orange blossom or even "milk flower" (whatever that might be, but it sounds so beautiful), and order it garnished with everything they've got.

Until you can get your hands on a cone or a cup full of Booza, I propose the humble Ice Cream Sandwich as a reliable vehicle of dessert happiness. You can probably find one right now, wherever you are. Even the paper-wrapped soft chocolate wafer with an angular brick of white ice cream found in the freezer case at the gas station can hit the spot in an emergency. Not only is the Ice Cream Sandwich a perfect technology, with no plastic spoons or cups to get between you and the refreshment, but it may also be an efficient way to expand your dessert flavor experience too.

If you find yourself at a good handmade ice cream shop, consider choosing an unusual cookie, like one I saw recently made with crisped rice and purple ube; or white chocolate, macadamia nuts, and cranberries; or toffee, coffee, and pretzels. Contrast the cookie with up to three types of adventurous ice cream in

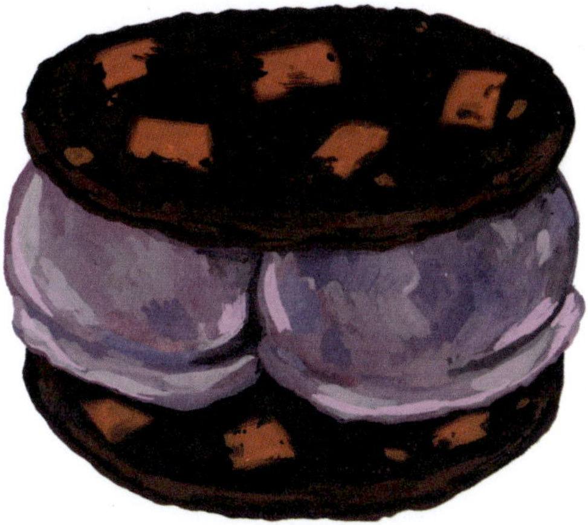

Chocolate and Salted-Caramel Cookie and Ube Ice Cream Sandwich

between. Imagine the profusion of flavors included in each scoop or half scoop of ice cream containing, say, black milk tea with bouncy boba pearls; ricotta, rosemary, and lemon zest; or rose, lychee, and raspberry swirls. I've even found an elegant Ice Cream Sandwich combination that was described as a whole *cheese course*, containing olive oil, figs, blue cheese, walnuts, and port wine! By fanciful Ice Cream Sandwich math (isn't this the best kind of math?), I figure you could taste up to thirteen significant flavors at once, in wild conversational contrasts and harmonies, in just one perfect handful of dessert.

BUBBLE TEA

My addiction to Bubble Tea has long been in development. I tasted my very first one twenty years ago and remember it vividly—a hot, jasmine-scented Chinese tea whipped together with a raw egg yolk. It was served from a kiosk in Taipei, where Bubble Tea was invented in the 1980s. With immigrants from the region settling around Asia, in the western United States, and elsewhere, Bubble Tea in all its indulgent and imaginative variations has since become omnipresent in globalized cities around the world.

Wildly inventive, sometimes luxurious, Bubble Tea is a wonderful concoction. Whether you are craving something creamy and warm in winter, or fruity, sweet, and slush-cold in summer—or even something clarifying before an exam—there is a mixed Bubble Tea to satisfy all your whims. Each one will be chock-full of sugar, cream, caffeine, or even *candy*, if your situation is urgent. While I am quite committed to my fail-safe order (black milk tea with 0% sugar and boba), the last drink I tried (for research purposes, of course) was layered with syrupy

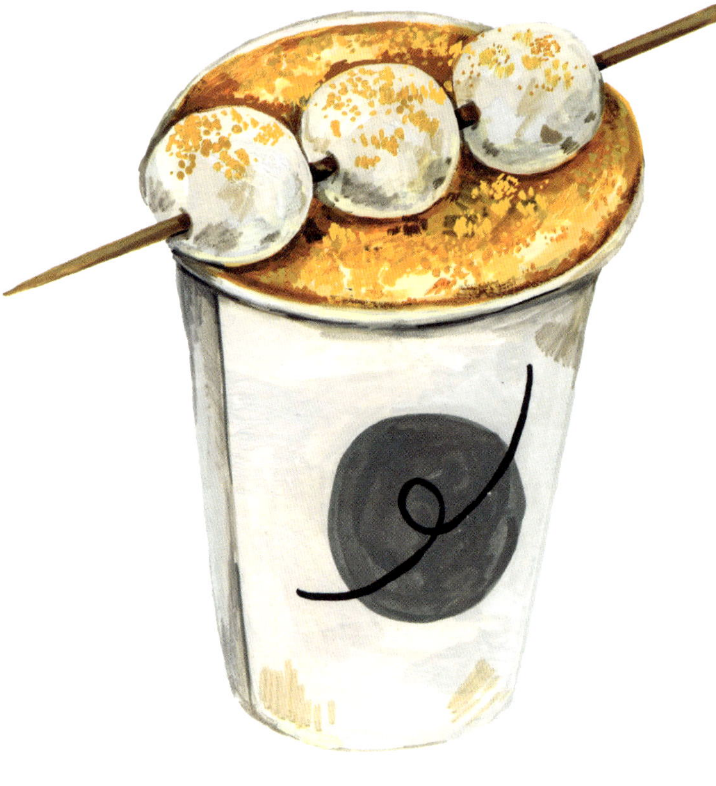

Torched Custard Black Milk Tea with Mochi and Kinako Powder

brown sugar pearls, matcha whipped creamily together with milk, and a thick caramelized cap of freshly torched egg custard. The moment I pushed my straw through the still-warm custard into the cold tea and ice and down into the warm boba, I was already weighing the impression I would make if I were to drink it all up and promptly order another.

I think of Bubble Tea as the tea lover's antidote to feeling left out of café culture's obsession with foamy, bespoke coffee drinks. For a *tea*-totaler, a Bubble Tea is as extravagant a grown-up treat as a fruity, umbrella-garnished mai tai. And even though it can go for up to $10 a cup, Bubble Tea is almost a bargain compared to the cost of an upmarket urban cocktail. Plus, it's assembled with care just for you.

My first, most important tip for a good Bubble Tea experience is that you find a shop that uses quality tea and natural flavorings. First, look at the color of their matcha drinks. Matcha should be a light lime green and not a grayish or murky-tank green scooped from a large plastic tub in a sunny window. Second, check out the ingredients behind the counter and look for real fruit rather than bins of artificial powdered flavorings. Together, these are good signs. Stale, improperly brewed tea will taste like a cup of used dishwater, made worse by the nondairy creamer and chemical flavoring stirred into it. You might also spot a higher-end shop by their choice to brew fine Chinese and Japanese teas and to forgo the extravagant candy toppings in favor of a few traditional embellishments,

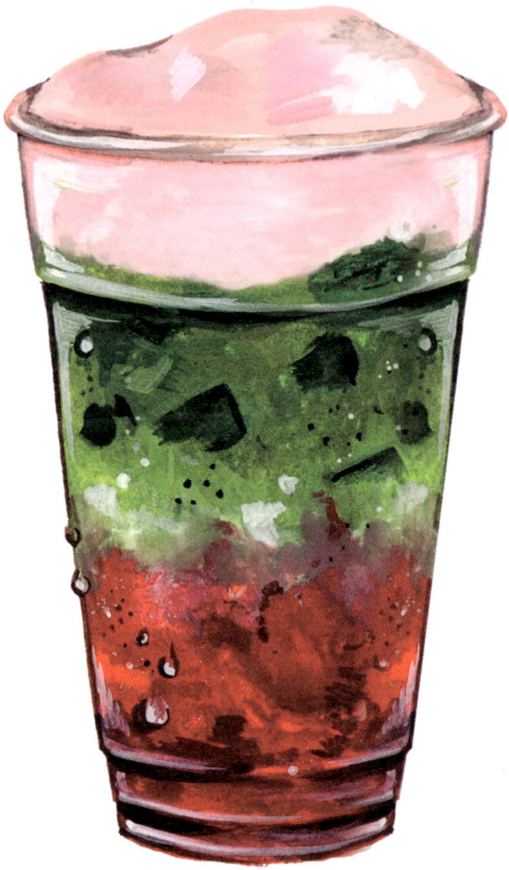

Strawberry Matcha Bubble Tea with Strawberry Foam

embellishments, like red bean paste or grass jelly, added in tastefully elegant layers.

If you find yourself in a city, even a small one, with a significant East Asian diasporic community, particularly of the college student variety, you are almost guaranteed to find a Bubble Tea shop nearby. Unless you are a savvy teenager or have one with you to be your translator and ordering guide, you may find the expansive menus overwhelming. They might feature various hot, cold, milky, flavored, and even coffee varieties, multiplied by the dozens of possible combinations among flavorings, sugar levels, and toppings. The permutations of your drink order are endlessly customizable, right down to the precise percentage of sugar you prefer in your lotus seed oolong cheese foam or taro boba slush.

To help you make your order, the next two pages offer a quick guide to common terms, flavors, and toppings.

TEA TERMS

BLACK TEA: Fully oxidized tea, sometimes known as English tea or malty breakfast tea, usually served with milk, described as *black milk tea* or *Hokkaido milk tea* in shops.

GREEN TEA: Pale-colored tea with a refreshing grassy or vegetal flavor, sometimes jasmine-scented, often served in shops with natural juice, fruit, or powdered fruit flavors.

OOLONG TEA: Fine pale-colored tea (often from Taiwan), partly oxidized, with a flowery fragrance and aftertaste, usually served clear like green tea with the addition of fruit flavors and/or honey.

AGED TEA: Aged or fermented pu-erh tea, leathery, tasting mildly of the barnyard, with rich notes like black tea. While it's untraditional to mix it with milk, it is delicious in milky Bubble Tea.

ROASTED TEA: Either genmaicha tea, a comforting green tea blended with whole grains of roasted rice, or hojicha tea—a toasty, roasted green tea (as close as tea might get to the flavor of coffee) that can be powdered and is good for lattes.

MATCHA TEA: Powdered Japanese green tea, very high in caffeine (not for kids!), with an umami and fresh grassy taste. Takes well to milk; served with sugar, or without for a more grown-up beverage. Order a matcha milk tea, a matcha slush, or a matcha latte.

FLAVORS

FRUIT: Mango, coconut, pineapple, kumquat, soursop, melon, creamy green avocado, pungent slippery durian, and many others.

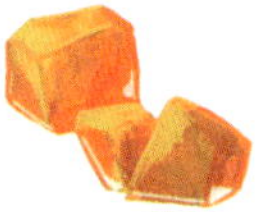

BUTTERFLY PEA: A natural flavor from the Thai sweet pea flower that tastes a little like wheatgrass and colors your tea a natural, startling paint-box blue.

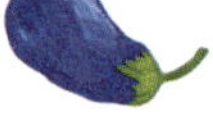

UBE: A richly purple potato, like taro (discussed later).

HIBISCUS: Tart and red, and, like jasmine, this flowery tea is great mixed into cold, clear green and oolong teas in the summer.

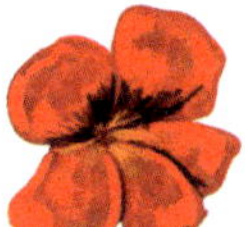

TOPPINGS

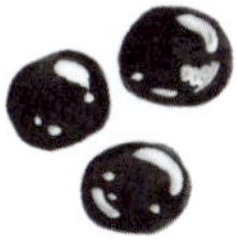

BOBA: Pea-size chewy spheres or "pearls" made with tapioca flour. They sometimes come in different flavors (like brown sugar or black sesame) and colors, though typically they're plain black or clear. Crystal boba are usually translucent, irregular, and white; they're made from agar and gelatin and have a slightly softer texture than regular boba. Popping boba, which are popular with kids, are made with a thin skin of seaweed extract and burst with syrupy juice in your mouth.

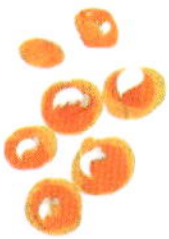

SAGO: Tiny pearls made from sago palm starch that add a slippery texture to your drink and absorb surrounding flavors.

CHEESE FOAM: A frothy, savory blend of milk ingredients and cream cheese.

TORCHED CUSTARD: Like the best part of a crème brûlée on top of your Bubble Tea.

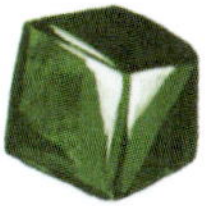

GRASS JELLY: Silky, gelatinous cubes of herbaceous green jelly. Also popular are flavored coconut jelly and multicolored, fruity rainbow jelly.

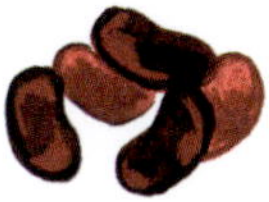

RED BEAN: Sweetened azuki bean paste common in many traditional East Asian desserts.

QQ: Usually a combination of two toppings, especially boba and coconut jelly.

BASIL SEED: Small black seeds from the tulsi (holy basil) plant that become gelatinous (like chia seeds do) when mixed with liquid.

TARO: A purple root vegetable with a mild, vanilla-like flavor and sweetness. If you would like to try a sensational-looking purple Bubble Tea, you might also order ube flavor, or ask for purple potato.

FRESH FRUIT: Mango, grapefruit, coconut, and passionfruit are popular, along with many others. Try the flavor that is currently trending in several cities, a green matcha milk tea layered with a pretty, red strawberry compote.

Order your tea style (with milk if desired) and flavorings (if any), and indicate if you would like your tea slushy, cold, or hot. While it might seem excessive to ask for so many specific modifications, it is the rule to also state your preferred ice level (no ice, less ice, regular ice, or extra ice) and sugar level (0%, 30%, 50%, etc.) at the register. Bubble Teas can run as sweet as an ice cream sundae, so it's fortunate that sugar levels can be reduced to taste. Then ask for your preferred toppings, usually one or two. If you like, you can simply say "QQ" like a pro, or take the easy way and just point to one of the "signature" drinks illustrated on a nearby poster, with many of these variables already predetermined for you.

One final note for those drinking Bubble Tea with young children: Remember that despite the colorful, candy-like enticements, all *Camellia sinensis* leaf teas contain caffeine. Also, chewy, slippery boba pearls can pose a choking hazard, especially when sucked up unpredictably through a wide straw. If you would like to share a Bubble Tea with kids, be mindful of ordering only caffeine-free or low-caffeine fruit teas or juices, and consider ordering jellies, beans, custards, popping boba, or other toppings that might be easier to swallow than boba, but just as fun.

At any age, enjoy the first moment of your Bubble Tea drinking experience: Boldly thrust the angle-edged straw through the plastic top on your sealed cup with a spectacular, piercing *CRACK!*

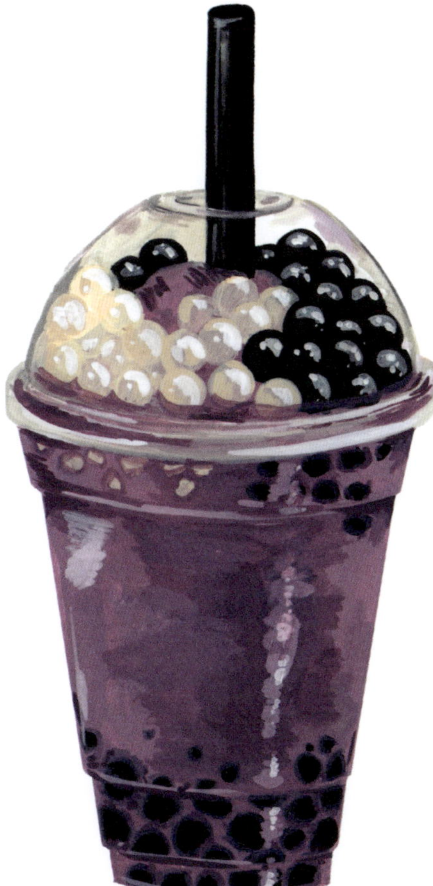

Taro Milk Bubble Tea with Black and White Pearls

Bubble Waffle Hotdog & Bacon Donut

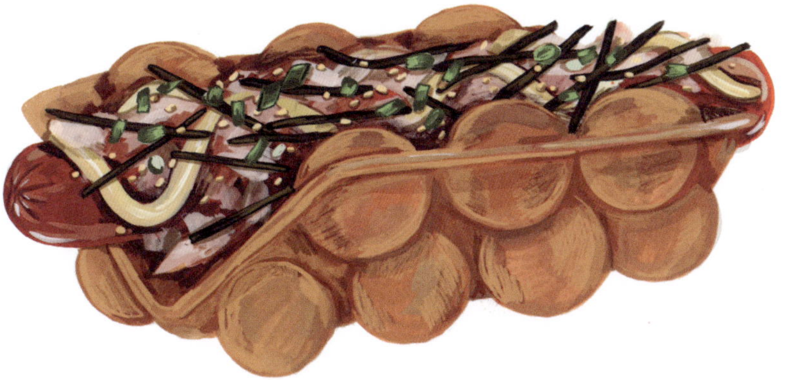

Bubble Waffle Hotdog in the "Jappa" Style

I skipped breakfast this morning, and with my grumbling stomach, all I can think of as I write at the public library is how much I would give to be handed a Bubble Waffle Hotdog right now. Can you imagine a hot, crisp bubble waffle fresh off the griddle, wrapped around a hot dog and topped with a blizzard of irresistible Japanese-style garnishes? What a meal! And I can hardly think of anything messier—or a more effective obstacle to getting my work done—than eating a Bubble Waffle Hotdog over a laptop in the library.

Garnished with fluttery fish flakes, tempura bits, ketchup, mayo honey mustard, and seaweed, a Bubble Waffle Hotdog is both East and West; sweet and salty; junky and fancy; breakfast and dinner *and* dessert, gloriously all at once.

I wanted to include something savory in this book, a surprise borderline dessert, if you count it as dessert at all. I chose the Bubble Waffle Hotdog because it's fun, containing a universe of unnecessary pleasures, and also because it's uncommon enough to benefit from some official encouragement to find one. In my city, crisp waffles like these are sometimes called *Hong Kong* or *egg waffles*, and the specific combination of waffle and wiener is sometimes called a *Japa-dog*. While there are various other combinations of hot dogs with similar garnishes—smothered in yakisoba noodles or shrimp tempura or gobs of chili or cheese—I'm going to recommend this one specific umami explosion. And my dream is that this rapturous ode might boost popular demand and make them more available for all of us.

If you struggle to find a Bubble Waffle Hotdog, try to meet your specific savory-pork-plus-dessert cravings with some other treat that features bacon as a key ingredient. I've seen Elvis Presley's famous peanut butter, banana, and bacon sandwich taken as inspiration for donuts and other sweets. There are maple syrup and bacon-flavored chocolates and ice cream sundaes too. I can't forget a Bacon Donut I tasted with my family in Tokyo, made with thick slabs of salty, smoky pork belly

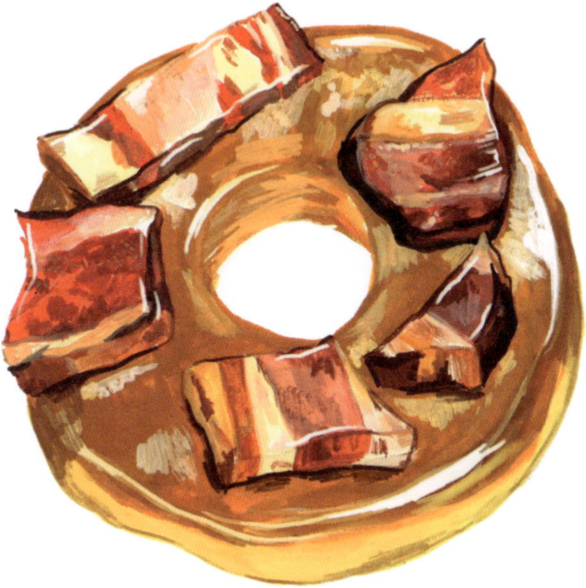

Bacon Donut

embedded in a pearlescent sugar glaze. It had a kind of indecent beauty, a repulsive-attractant among dessert species. Mostly it was an attractant.

Except for vegetarians (so sorry!) and for a few of you whose religious beliefs might exclude it, I urge you to taste one of these sweet and savory enticements. While they satisfy so many desires at once, they couldn't be easier to messily demolish.

CANELÉ

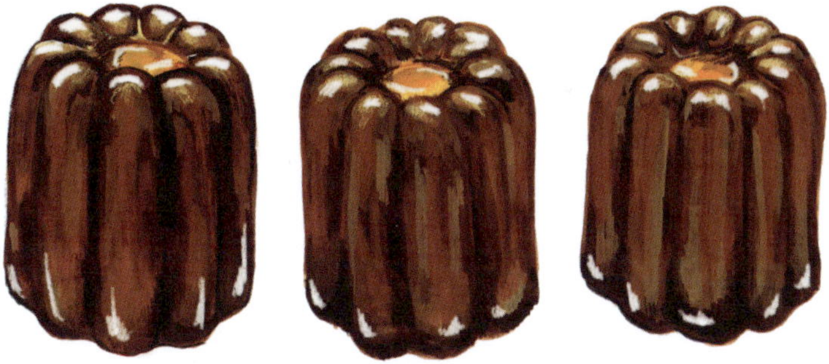

Canelés

These shiny, fluted domes gleam irresistibly at me from behind patisserie counters, and by now I confess I may have ordered and eaten at least a hundred of them.

A properly made Canelé is a small, eggy French cake, scented with vanilla and rum, that looks smoothly burnished and glows from within. Its form is somewhere between a sandcastle and a Bundt cake, with regular undulations that expand the surface area of a chewy, nearly burnt sweet crust. This contrasts with a moist, custardy interior. A Canelé is composed of the most basic ingredients (just eggs, flour, sugar, vanilla, rum, milk, and butter), but these ingredients are manipulated with a physicist's precision in a dynamic interplay among heat, batter, metal, tradition, and time. The result has a uniquely warming, rummy aroma and produces dueling, infinitely satisfying sensations in your mouth.

Without any qualifications whatsoever in French historic pastry technology, I attempted to bake Canelés at home. I followed all the fussiest instructions for the two-day process. I melted butter, rested batter, painted specialized molds with beeswax, and wrangled precise and aggressive temperature adjustments. After all of that, I successfully produced little blackened cakes that were cemented to the pan so hard that I had to indelicately pry them out with a fork. This is why you should leave some things to the experts! Go buy some nice Canelés where they know exactly what they are doing. It's just not worth the trouble to try to make them, even if you do get to eat all the craggy, messy shards by yourself.

I am glad I can gratify my Canelé cravings instantly now, as the treat has become a staple in the dessert cases of fashionable French bakeries everywhere. While my favorite way to enjoy one is warm and fresh and plain, I've noticed that specialty shops are emerging that are entirely dedicated to the prim little cakes. Like a selection of fancier iced donuts, they are sometimes available in a range of flavors—including lemon, Earl Grey tea, salted caramel, blood orange, and coffee. Once, in Japan, I even saw one flavored with wormwood! In these specialty shops, Canelés are daintily garnished, and when you order one to go, your perfect dessert will be packaged like a precious, fragile ornament.

Cannoli

In the truly moving YouTube series called *Pasta Grannies*, grandmothers from across regions of Italy are recorded making fresh pasta, ravioli, gnocchi, carnival sweets, and traditional Easter lunches. They are doing the work they've performed nearly every day for decades, memorized by their muscles and their bones. In an interview with Sarah Ubertaccio on the q.b. Cucina website, Vicky Bennison, founder of the online archive, explains, "I just thought, someone has to make a record of this. It's the passing of a generation."[3]

In one typical episode, we meet 93-year-old Clara in her kitchen in Sicily. She starts with a rolling pin and two pasta machines to muscle through Cannoli dough made with type 00 flour, fat, sugar, and vinegar "to get more bubbles." After dozens of ovals of dough have rested on a clean flour-covered tablecloth, she dips her fingertips into a dish of water, then wraps the Cannoli around short bamboo canes that she has harvested from her own garden. Everything (including the bamboo) goes into a fryer full of bubbling lard. When the crackling, golden pastry is cooled and firm, Clara uses a butter knife to patiently fill each tube with a ricotta and chocolate filling.

Bennison's channel has appealed to me (and so many others) not just because I no longer have a Cannoli-making nonna in my life, but because these videos connect me to elder generations and some of their most caring teachings, along with food ingredients that remind me of a beloved place, sunshine, and home.

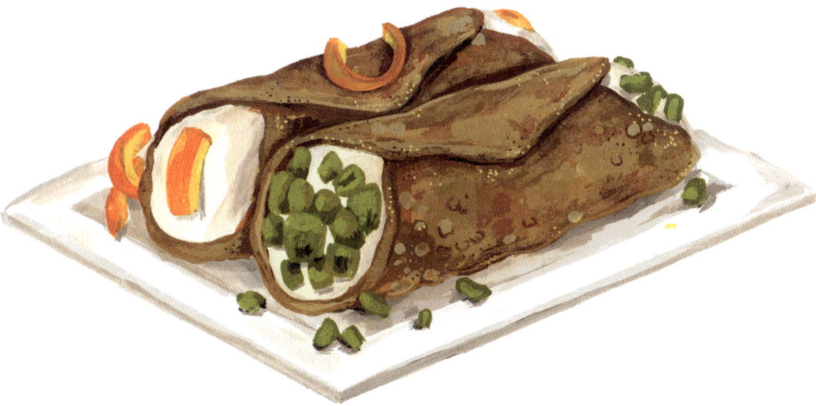

Cannoli with Pistachio and Candied Orange

My favorite part of the Cannoli video is when Clara urges a handsome Italian man on set to taste a fresh, crunchy, creamy pastry immediately. He bites and chews and pauses for a heavy moment. Then his eyes roll up with bliss (can he see into heaven?), and for an instant, he seems upset with Clara, for so utterly undoing him. "Buonissimo!" he declares, while squeezing his hands together and shaking them, as if he is experiencing so much feeling that he is struggling to hold it all up.

Good crunchy Cannoli can be found anywhere there are Italians and Italian foods (particularly from Southern Italy). Fortunately for the world, that means almost everywhere. While chocolate chips, lemon zest, cinnamon, and other adornments are common, I like the Cannoli made with a mix of mascarpone and ricotta, topped with pistachios and tailed with candied orange peel. A little bakery sleuthing may be in order before you find the combination of flavors you like from a place that fills the crisp shells upon ordering, or frequently throughout the day. "Best Cannoli" lists are not unheard of in many major cities, and life-altering pastry should not be hard to find. Eat yours fast and fresh and gratefully. Otherwise, Nonna (real or imagined) will be disappointed, and your Cannoli will be soggy.

Charcoal Ice Cream

It's an unlikely pairing: ice-cold milk stirred together with jet-black char. Of all the contemporary things colored by activated charcoal, from bottled water to face creams, cocktails to pizza dough, ice cream is probably the most startling. It is both elemental in form and otherworldly in appearance. We don't eat many pure-black foods, apart from licorice or things burned unintentionally. But a swirling charcoal soft serve, especially in an inky-black waffle cone, is unabashedly surprising. And eating one, tall and spirally as a unicorn horn, is less an act of nourishment than a kind of performance art.

But is it natural? Is it even food? When I looked more deeply into the black food trend, I learned that activated charcoal is made of heated, carbonized coconut husks—less threatening than, say, ice cream amended with barbecue briquettes. On the one hand, health influencers and celebrities swear by charcoal's ability to clean drinking water, cure hangovers, and absorb toxins in the body—among them, some suggest, even *spider venom*! Mainstream health professionals are more circumspect about these claims. While charcoal is absorbent, it turns out that it doesn't discriminate among, say, last night's excess alcohol, nutrients vital to your survival, and prescription medication.

Black charcoal flavoring is banned in New York and presumably in other places too, though this isn't always enforced. But since health professionals are only wary of the additive if it's taken in large quantities or very often, it seems harmless enough to try it once. I asked the staff at my own local Charcoal Ice Cream

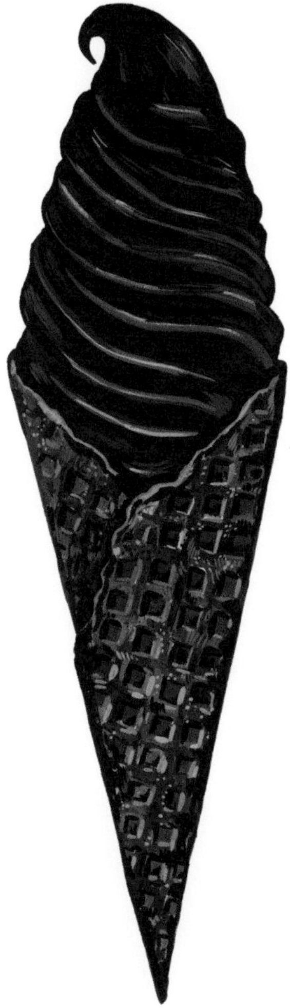

Charcoal Ice Cream in a Charcoal Cone

purveyor whether they have regulars who come back and eat the black ice cream all the time. They said that while there are a few, most customers are first-timers, taking snapshots of themselves in the act.

The flavor of Charcoal Ice Cream is subtler than you might expect, considering the drama of its appearance. Because the charcoal itself is tasteless, the ice cream I tried was flavored delicately with coconut. Some shops make their black ice cream taste like vanilla or lemon, for surprise or contrast, and swirl it together with other unusual ice cream flavors like pandan (an herbaceous green leaf) or ube (a bright purple yam). Overall, black soft serve is mild, smooth on the palate, and refreshing. However, remember to smile at your friends and take your selfie *before* you lick—because the charcoal will temporarily leave a ghoulish gray stain all over your teeth.

CHOCOLATE SHOT & LAVA CAKE

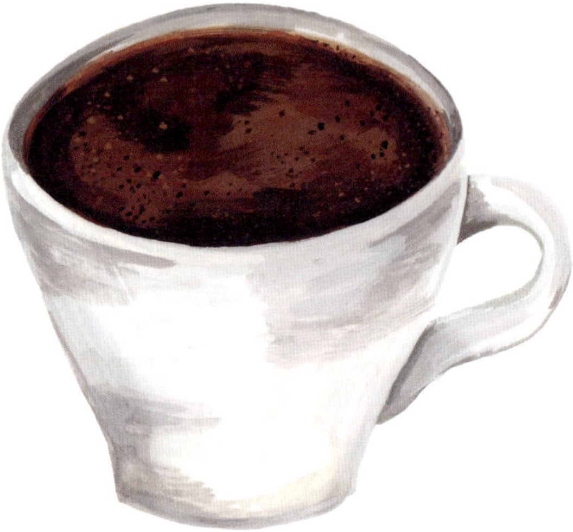

Chocolate Shot

Of all the chocolate desserts I can think of, none is as satisfyingly pure an encounter as the Chocolate Shot. Unlike the kind of thin hot chocolate you might be offered at the skating rink cafeteria, all gritty with crystals, a proper Chocolate Shot is a dose of serious medicine. It might even be a cure for everything! At best it's made of the purest and most potent chocolate available and served thick as the molten middle of a Lava Cake in a very small cup.

If you are going to have chocolate in this form, unadorned by little dehydrated marshmallows (or even milk), you need to be as fussy about its quality as possible. And since mass-produced, cheap chocolate is notoriously implicated in exploitative labor practices—not just historically, but still to this day—fair-trade and ethically sourced ingredients *feel* better, as well as taste better. Find a dedicated shop that serves chocolate, Chocolate Shots, and little else. Ideally, they should specialize in making bars and truffles from scratch, going so far as to ferment, roast, crack, grind, and conch out the cacao beans themselves. Explicit references to cacao percentages, chocolate-growing regions (like Madagascar, Peru, and Ecuador), and forms of rarer cacao varietals, like Criollo or Trinitario, are all good indicators that you are in a place that cares about fine ingredients. Ask your chocolate seller just how good their ingredients really are, and if necessary be ready to pay the higher cost.

When chocolate is good, tasting of tannins, earth, nuts, dried fruit, and wood, among many other complex flavors, it is a profoundly moving substance. This chocolate contains concentrated stimulants that mimic the body's own neurotransmitters, like dopamine and adrenaline, and that can actually raise your blood pressure and heart rate. In my experience, just one sip of a Chocolate Shot—nearly clotted, body-warm, and concentrated—is enough to inspire an immediate rush. I can feel the tingly buzz of it surging through my bloodstream and reddening my cheeks—especially if I'm a little hungry and have deprived myself of sugar (or any cheap chocolate) for a few days.

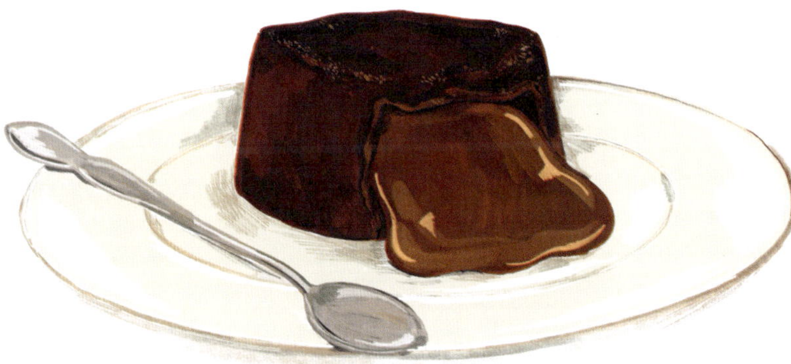

Chocolate Lava Cake

I recommend preparing for a high-quality Chocolate Shot by building up a craving for it this way, to wring as much pleasure from the experience as possible.

You might also find a good Chocolate Shot flavored with natural amendments like gianduja (hazelnut) and orange zest. Or enjoy it spiced provocatively with chili peppers, inspired by the bitter, sacred drink of the ancient Mayas, who were among the first to grow, roast, and grind the chocolhaa. They drank it as an aphrodisiac, traded it as precious currency, and revered it—as we might too if we had just the right communion with it in its ideal form.

*

Speaking of Lava Cake, this steaming joy in a bit of crockery is ubiquitous on restaurant dessert menus for a reason. It exists in the spongy zone between cake and soufflé, cooked and uncooked, solid and liquid chocolate. While the ingredients are simple, Lava Cake is notoriously hard to get just right at home. Ideally, a Lave Cake is eaten straight from the oven while the edges are toasty and the center is fluid, shiny, and warm. One greeting from your spoon should see the cake releasing molten chocolate all over your plate, before it dribbles down your wrist and finally your chin. When it's great, with a little cream or a contrasting slice of strawberry, this is one of the most obvious reasons that one should never miss an opportunity to order dessert.

Coconut Jellies & Sweet Corn, Tapioca, and Coconut Pudding

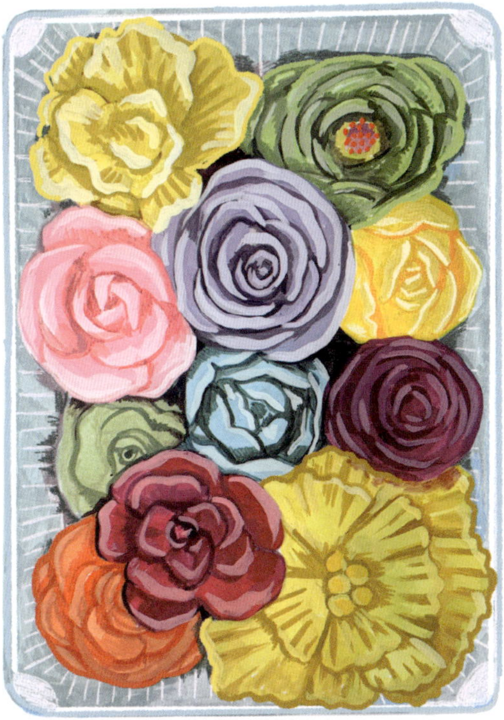

Thai Coconut Jelly Flowers

How could I resist a box of elaborate, colorful, edible blooms? And the ones I tasted were no less stunning after bumping through rush-hour traffic, strapped to the rack of a commuter bicycle. When I finally got the container of Coconut Jellies in my hands and set them next to a steeping pot of jasmine tea (a delicate spring oolong would also have been appropriate), they looked vivid, dewy, and hand-carved, petal by petal. Each gelatinous flower was so surprisingly sturdy that you might even say they were *snappy.* When I could finally bear to nibble one, it tasted strongly of coconut and sweetness. It's true these were not the most nuanced or complex in flavor, but some things—like wobbly yellow chrysanthemums, flirtatious lavender tulips, and delicately modeled pink roses—are so beautiful to behold, I must insist on the whole experience anyway.

Wherever you can buy Southeast Asian foods, you will find some of the prettiest and most colorful desserts in the world. Seek out restaurants and bakeries inspired by the culinary traditions of countries like Thailand, Vietnam, Malaysia, Indonesia, and the Philippines. Many of these hot, vibrant regions offer similar sweet treats made with coconut milk and agar, which is a clear, plant-based gelatin. Look for cubes, spheres, cast leaves, and blooms, like my Coconut Jellies, which came from a Thai pastry shop, or striking cakes, which look as if they have been layered with sheets of colorful stained glass.

Even though a Sweet Corn, Tapioca, and Coconut Pudding is considerably less showy than elaborate jelly blooms, this Southeast Asian dessert dazzles me with its sweet and salty tangle of flavors, textures, and aromas. You might find it made into a milky bowl of cold dessert soup, with rice-size pieces of watery young coconut and swimming with chewy pearls. But the nicest way I have found this dessert is in a palm-size

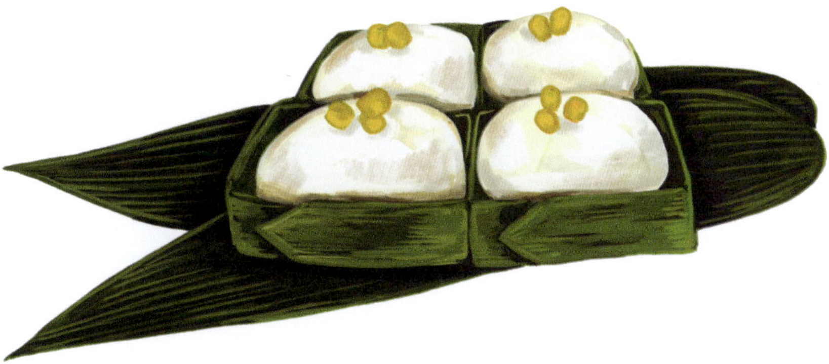

Sweet Corn, Tapioca, and Coconut Pudding

pandan leaf boat, garnished with a sweet yellow corn kernel atop a savory coconut cream.

Pandan leaves have become trendy outside of Southeast Asia for a reason, so be alert to this special tropical garnish and flavoring, which imparts an extra flowery, caramel-like perfume to desserts. It adds new dimensions of luxuriousness (at least in my own chilly North American city) to cakes, jellies, ice creams, and puddings. It also colors them a brilliant, emerald green.

CREPE CAKE

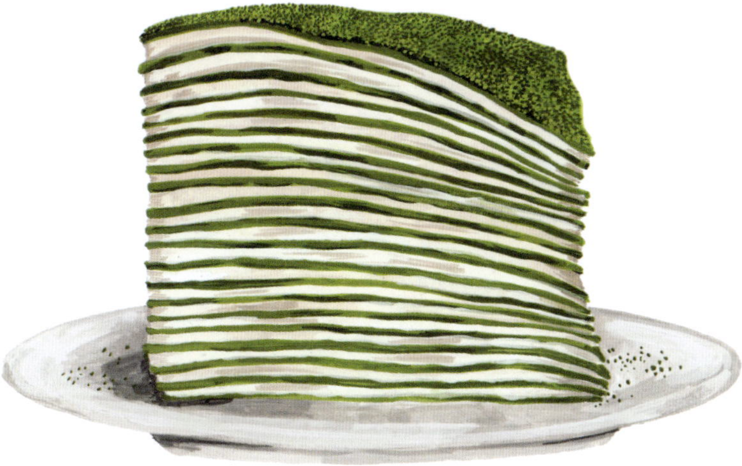

Matcha Crepe Cake

When I see a Crepe Cake, stacked impossibly neatly and mortared together with cream, I remember the specific sensation of cutting through the twenty, thirty, or even forty layers of paper-thin crepes. It's like running a delicate mallet across the length of a xylophone. This is a striking, graphic dessert, combining delicate flavors and textures, all about to play percussion in my mouth.

After tasting a perfect triangle of matcha-flavored Crepe Cake from the eye-boggling frozen sweets section of my favorite Chinese grocery chain, I learned this particular dessert represents more than a passing trend. It turns out Crepe Cakes are increasingly available from cafés and supermarkets everywhere and are very much worth exploring in all their possible cultural iterations and flavors. You might find a French one layered with mousse and iced with chocolate ganache, or a shortcake-inspired slice made with sliver-thin strawberries tucked into all the layers of cream. Another playful Crepe Cake might surprise you with a pretty spectrum of rainbow-colored layers, revealing themselves only after you slice into it. What is your favorite flavor? There is inevitably a Crepe Cake for you, made with everything from salted caramel to lemon curd, or even durian fruit in a pungent green-tinted sponge.

One thing I don't recommend is trying to create this technical wonder at home! My own attempt—an irregular Frankenstein version—was nothing like the posh vanilla Crepe Cake I tasted at the trendy Lady M Cake bakery chain in New York. This shop is famous for selling a range of cakes with impossibly thin layers of tender crepes laid upon impossibly thin layers of cold whipped cream, until they have produced a hard-edged, modernist confection with equidistant stripes. It's no wonder the line stretches past the length of the counter and way out the door. The all-white, starkly designed boutique I visited in Manhattan looked more like a Soho commercial art gallery than a bakery. By the time my turn came to receive one slice of Crepe Cake, packaged in an opulent, monogrammed box, I felt as if I had acquired a masterpiece.

Cupcake with Buttercream

Only at Magnolia Bakery in Manhattan will you find cupcakes so famous they are guarded by a bouncer. More than twenty years ago, the New York bakery made an appearance on an episode of *Sex and the City*: Carrie Bradshaw dished about a new crush while peeling crinkled parchment from the base of an adorable Cupcake with Buttercream and licking frosting from her fingertips. Lines packed with both television and cupcake fans have stretched down the block ever since. *Cupcakes!* everyone must have been thinking. *How could we have forgotten*?

The good news is that in almost any city you will find a place that makes great cupcakes. Maybe it's a mom-and-pop shop that resembles the neighborhood bakeries of a certain kind of childhood, smelling of all the smells and stirring up memories and their commensurate emotions. Or you might spot a contemporary affair in a white cube space, with stylish cupcakes in a glass case. No matter where they are sold, cupcakes are likely to come in a crowd-pleasing selection of flavors, garnished with chunks of caramel or chocolate, snowfalls of coconut, tints of raspberries or lemons and their zests, or a joyful explosion of sprinkles. Look for the signature high, whimsical swirl of buttercream frosting expertly piped on top.

Don't be tempted to crack the base of the cupcake and put it on top of your frosting to make a hasty, tidier sandwich. I know some people do this, but isn't the whole point of a cupcake its excess, its too-muchness? It *should* be too tall and too full of sweet fluffs of frosting without enough counterbalancing cake,

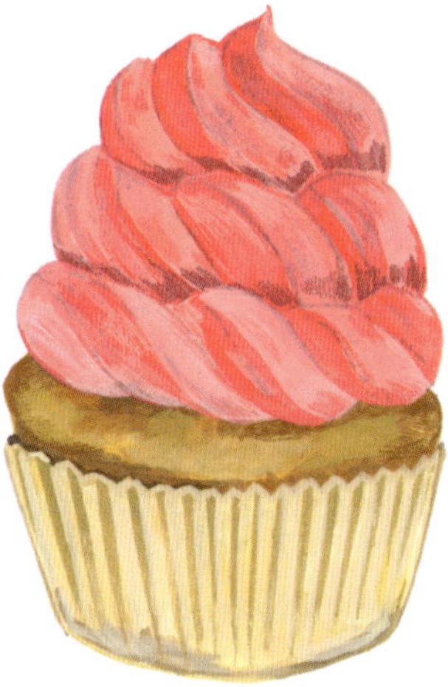

Vanilla Cupcake with Raspberry Buttercream

and it should be made with too-white flour and have absolutely nothing wholesome about it. The best cupcake is messy and, just like on TV, gives you something to lick off your chin and the tip of your nose and all your fingers. A cupcake should be so big and unwieldy you feel five years old, which was likely the last time you wanted to press your whole face into a birthday cake—or at least the last time you did.

Sharing a large cake in a gesture of celebration and ceremony is very special. A cupcake, though, is for any day, and it's all yours. You can probably go out and get one right now, in a flavor you love, with a shockingly disproportionate amount of butter-cream. A cupcake is like a sweetened cloud, and you get to float away on it.

Éclair & Cream Puff

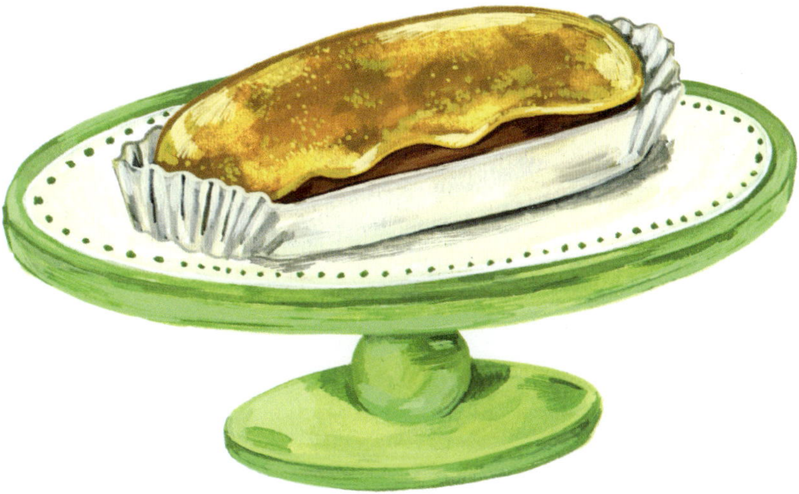

Gold-Plated Hazelnut Dacquoise Éclair

A classic Éclair, made since the early 19th century in France, is a simple, soft, and crunchy pastry sandwich, filled with vanilla custard and topped with chocolate ganache. *Éclair* translates directly to "flash of lightning," and there is some debate about whether this refers to the sheen of the long streak of chocolate glaze or, more likely, how quickly these light, irresistible pastries disappear.

While you might see something that looks like a long, creamy Éclair at almost any neighborhood donut shop, it's worth doing a little research to find a true choux-based confection (so many donut shops sell Éclair-shaped donuts) and the freshest and nicest one in your city. While you want a well-made one, don't be fooled by too much surface glamour! The specialty Éclair shop in the most fashionable urban neighborhood may look like the right kind of place, with an elegant spread of slim Éclairs in flavors like gluten-free chocolate joconde sponge, vanilla bean crème brûlée, blueberry-violet, passion fruit crémeux, and soft caramel. But the showy, gold-burnished hazelnut dacquoise that I ordered was surprisingly cold, dense, and airless. The choux pastry was mushy from too much time mingling with the chocolate-flavored custard filling, and I had the impression it had probably been made a few days before. Cue the fainting pâtissier!

Seek out a good French bakery that makes Éclairs fresh every day and with pride. I should have visited a different local place I know, which is much less flashy in presentation and more limited in flavorings. They wait to pipe your Éclair until after you order, crafting a just-right ratio of nearly sugarless, airy, crunchy choux to sweet, vanilla seed-flecked cream.

Until you find your own perfect Éclair, join me in a fantasy by watching one of the mesmerizing YouTube videos of specialty Éclair baker Romain Luyat, based in Lyon, who prepares at least five hundred perfect pastries every day. See him haul

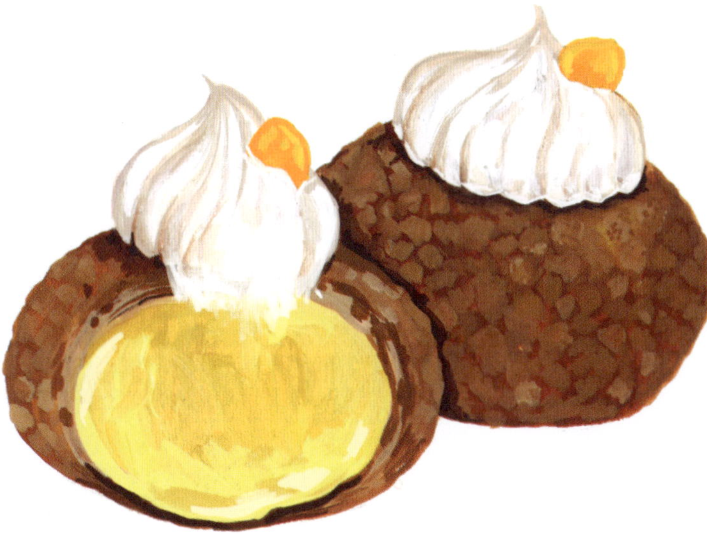

Lemon Cream Puffs with Craquelin

slabs of pale French butter the size of firewood into a pot, test the readiness of his batter by plunging his whole hand into the sticky mix, and perform the soothing work of piping the thick paste expertly into dozens of regular, slender batons. Once the pâte à choux comes out after a slow rise in the oven, and the chef beats a heavy custard with cream, he punctures and fills the inflated pastry. When everything is ready, watch him paint shiny stripes of red glaze back and forth along the length of each tinted choux until you are rapt. When you finally see the glorious result of his labors—Luyat's signature crimson praline Éclair, dotted with candied almonds—you, like me, might find your cheeks turning a matching shade of pink and your belly rumbling lasciviously.

In the absence of perfect Éclairs, it's a good thing that Cream Puffs are having a cultural moment. All around the cities I have visited in the last few years, I see shops specializing in freshly made, palm-size morsels of choux, stuffed to bursting with flavored cream. Some are frosted or dusted with icing sugar. Others are tantalizingly encrusted with the traditionally applied craquelin, a biscuity coating that doesn't quite fit the body of the choux, so it splits into a cracked, golden landscape that is as pretty as it is crisp. It's as if each of these baby Éclairs are made to fit perfectly into your mouth. This makes it possible, even mandatory, to help them fulfill their purpose by eating them all up.

Fat Bomb

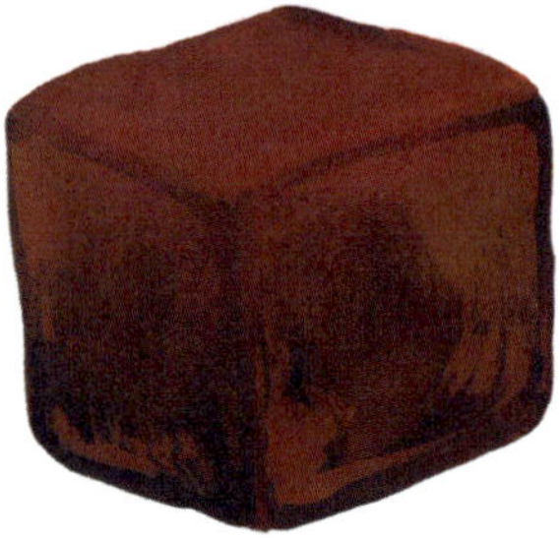

Chocolate Fat Bomb with Beet Powder

The hipster sauna and cold-plunge trend has come to my city, and the sunny café next door to the newest venue smells of essential oils, cedar, and the freshly anointed young patrons who work in the surrounding downtown culture district. In their form-fitting yoga clothes, they look like they are back from an exhilarating workout, or maybe they are just on their way? It's hard to tell, since everyone is glowing already.

Cafés like this sell celery slushies, chagaccinos, and something bewilderingly called *detox water*. But they usually also offer a selection of sweet treats for the ultra-health-conscious. Focusing on whole organic ingredients, these desserts tend to eschew dairy products, wheat flour, cane sugar, and other processed foods. Is there anything delicious left for a humble sweet tooth, you might be wondering? Apparently there is, though my mind spins trying to imagine all of the superfoods listed on their menu. How will spirulina, almond meal, hemp seeds, goji berries, protein powder, and maca taste all at once? I try not to worry when ordering anymore, and neither should you, since these slabs of dense nutrient-rich foods, rolled into coconut-covered balls or sectioned into tidy frosted squares, are going to be delicious. And probably virtuous.

Among these treats is something called a *Fat Bomb*—a hit with all of us who love the savory and sweet combination of peanut butter and chocolate. The Fat Bomb I ordered included nothing less than three kinds of tree nuts, pumpkin and sunflower seeds, various unusual powders and extracts, monk fruit, coconut, cinnamon, crunchy ground cacao nibs, and a coating of sugarless dark chocolate. And since there wasn't a trace of honey, dates, or anything else sweet in the whole long list, the entire super cube was dusted (brazenly!) with dehydrated powdered beets. I enjoyed the smooth texture of the cube, which felt like something between fudge and a solid piece of butter. I ate the Fat Bomb slowly, shoulders back, in the very grown-up, post-workout way one might savor fine chocolate. If you need a little more convincing, you can think of it less as a nugget of bitter health food and more as an elegant, extra-large truffle.

I recommend, however, that you do not make the mistake of carrying a few around all day, with the intention of devouring them later. *Bomb* is a good word for the explosion of leaking, liquefied, oily chocolate I found later all over the inside of my purse. Eat your own firm, fridge-cold Fat Bomb on the spot. And guess what? I hear if you can make it through a few of these dense, restorative, detoxifying desserts, then you don't really have to go to yoga.

FRUIT SANDO

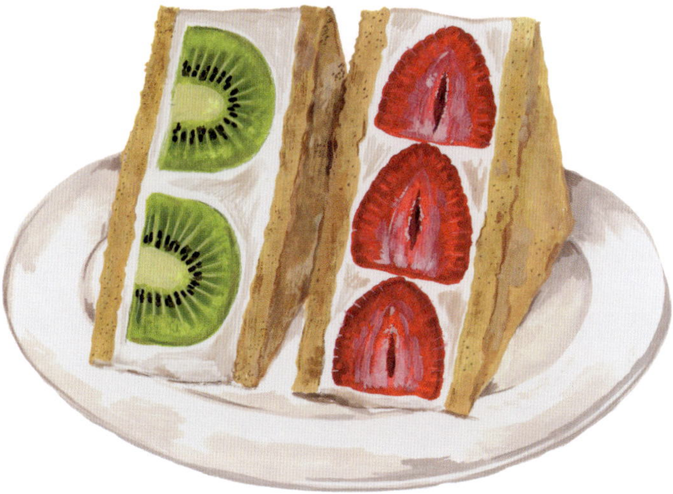

Fruit Sando with Kiwi and Strawberries

Fruit Sando is the anglicized name of the Japanese-style dessert sandwich typically made with soft milk bread, called *shokupan*, and filled with colorful fruit and whipped cream. You can find these wrapped tidily in cellophane in graceful Japanese fruit salons, which have served elegant parfaits, fruit-topped pancakes, and creamy sandwiches since the 1920s. You can also find the sandos in select urban cafés featuring Asian desserts, and if you are very lucky, you can even buy them from the refrigerated case at your local 7-Eleven.

Elyse Inamine describes the Fruit Sando as "a caricature of a dessert you'd dream up as a kid"[4] while confessing her obsession with them in *Bon Appétit* magazine. I agree this dessert might look fun and easy to make from only a few simple ingredients. But in fact, a proper Fruit Sando is made with great technical skill.

First, the shokupan dough must be risen and baked in a cubic pan until it is just done—fluffy and light as a feather duvet. Crusts are removed, and choice pieces of fruit are embedded into a stiff whipped cream in deliberate geometric patterns. Finally, to get the signature appearance of this dessert, the sandos are stacked and sliced through with a sharp blade. This makes precision edges out of soft bread and a clean cross section of surprising fruit jewels. Look for inventive or satisfyingly regular compositions of round green grapes and mandarin triangles, kiwi ovals radiant with seeds, and shining strawberry hearts. A Fruit Sando is like an art gallery for showcasing fruits as the precious things they are, in rainbow colors, illuminated against a backdrop of pure white bread and cream.

Now go ahead, bite into this pretty food. Enjoy the ensuing chaos of cream, fruit out of order, and drips and squishes and geometries asunder. You have ruined everything! Yet isn't perfection so delicious?

GULAB JAMUN

"It's too sweet!" is the familiar refrain of the dessert-phobe. Even though I expect to hear it, I laughed out loud recently, hearing my mom complain that even *honey* is "too sweet." She would never enjoy Indian desserts as much as I do, because many of my favorites, like Gulab Jamun, are literally soaking in it.

The soft, milk-powder balls of Gulab Jamun—like many traditional Indian sweets—are deep fried in ghee (clarified butter) before being soaked for several hours in a luscious honey or sugar syrup. The syrup can be scented with cardamom and rose, or sometimes vanilla, lemon, or saffron. The dumplings are spongy as donuts, and when they are done soaking, they are as juicy and sweet as the ripest peaches of your dreams. And they boast a unique textural bite that you might describe as squeaky, but Gulab Jamun aficionados call deliciously "squidgy."

Gulab Jamun is a popular dessert in South Asia, as well as everywhere around the world where there is a significant South Asian population, including in Britain, Canada, the United States, and the Caribbean. It is a joyful food served at South Asian weddings, at the Muslim holiday Eid, and at the Hindi festival of lights, Diwali, where families in their best new clothes enjoy wide copper platters of Gulab Jamun, steaming hot and floating in a shiny pool. Variously garnished with chopped nuts, rose petals, or flecks of silver leaf, they are the prettiest and most delectable orbs in a cosmos of syrup.

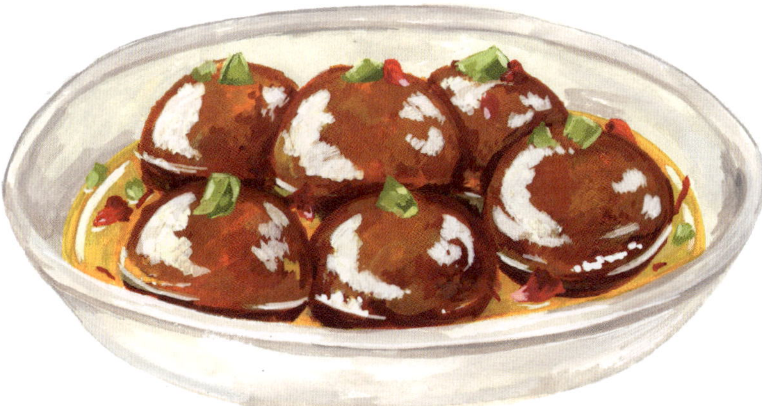

Gulab Jamun

Because I haven't been invited to this kind of party yet (hint, hint!), I've only ever found this dessert on the menu in Indian restaurants in Toronto. I eat it after a savory dosa pancake with a hot cup of chai. Indian and Pakistani grocery stores also often keep Gulab Jamun in a display case alongside glossy carrot halvah, nutty barfi, and swirls of fried jalebi—everything so sweet it makes your teeth tingle just to look at it all.

Even at the bargain curry place I always order from, a hot dish of three redolent dumplings brings a certain magic to the table. One dripping, spongy bite coats my mouth, throat, and chin with warm, oily deliciousness, a feeling of summery celebration so concentrated it's like a spoonful of dancing. A bite of Gulab Jamun feels to my world-worn palate like a sugar fast explosively broken. It is worth every immoderate, ecstatic bite.

HALO-
HALO

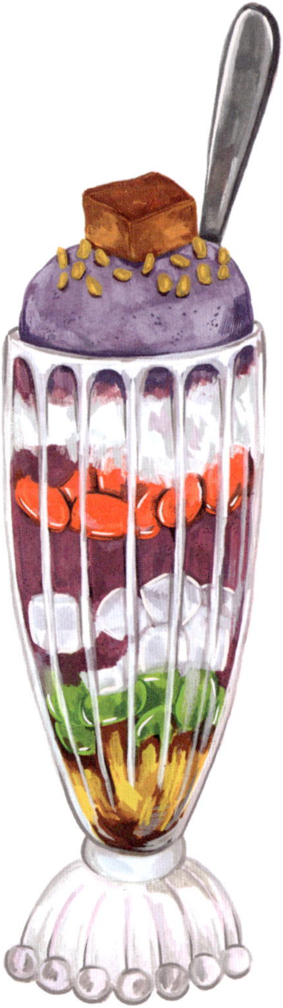

Halo-Halo

Among the best things I got from a youth spent in suburban Toronto Catholic schools were all the invitations to the homes of my Filipino friends. There, I inherited numerous aunties and grandmothers and sisters—all these titas and lolas and ates—who fed me rolled wafer cookies and peanut kisses, taught me songs on the piano, and once (with disastrously frizzy results) even home-permed my hair.

Because there are millions of Filipinos working and living outside of the Philippines—especially in Canada, the United States, the United Kingdom, the Middle East, Singapore, and Japan—there are also increasing numbers of Filipino amenities available in big cities around the world. Groceries, restaurants, food festivals, and parades offer some community and comfort to hardworking expats and their descendants. And since contemporary Filipino culture and fashion have been trending in big cities, popular treats like Halo-Halo are (thankfully!) more available than ever, for Filipinos and the rest of us, in between invitations to Tita's or Lola's or Ate's next house party.

Halo-Halo is an exuberant, colorful sundae made with a mound of fluffy shaved ice and a slew of chewy, syrupy, and creamy toppings. My friend Glicelle showed me the essentials when she unpacked an electric ice shaver, plus all the ingredients she had to carry to my house in a great big laundry basket. Halo-Halo typically includes red mung beans, white beans, silky jackfruit, chewy sugar palm fruit, coconut strings, and coconut jelly, all bathed in sugary syrup. These are topped with a sweet, cartoon-purple ube paste that Glicelle tells me her grandmother used to boil, mash, and strain herself to sell to all the neighbors before it was readily available in Toronto. On top of all these chunky garnishes are the dairy ingredients. First the spoonfuls of leche flan, a firm milk-and-egg custard in a pool of caramel and a direct inheritance from the Spanish colonists of the Philippines. And finally, the whole refreshing Halo-Halo is topped with generous lashings of evaporated milk, straight from the can.

Halo-halo means "mix mix" in Tagalog. This is what you do when it's presented to you in a tall showy glass: You take your spoon and mix all the colors and textures, ice and milk, into one chewy, slippery, gritty, sweet, and cooling slurry. If it's a special occasion, like a birthday or an anniversary or a celebration of friendship that has lasted steadily and lovingly over many years (thank you, Glicelle), you can even put a candle in it.

Ispahan

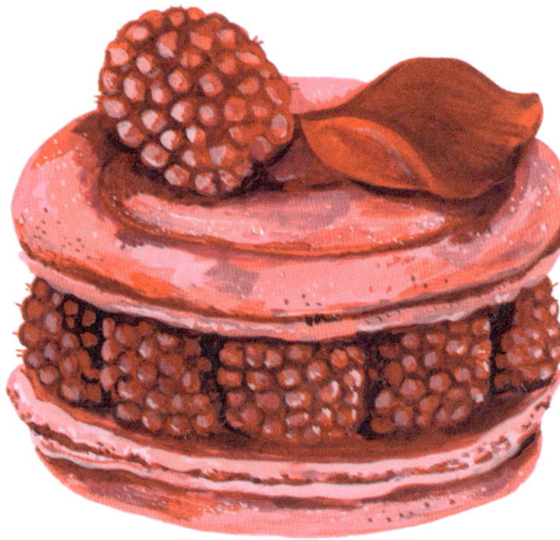

Ispahan

The first time I ate one, I didn't even know its whispery swoon of a name: *Ispahan*. I was first attracted to this exquisite dessert in an immaculate patisserie near the Luxembourg Gardens in Paris. It was developed after a decade of experimentation by the Alsatian pastry chef and inventor of modern French macarons, Pierre Hermé. Called by *Vogue* the "Picasso of Pastry," Hermé is known for presenting bold flavor combinations in gallery-like displays of technical perfection and pure panache. This one is named for the strongly scented, pink damask Rose d'Ispahan, which itself was named for the Iranian town Isfahan, renowned for blooming gardens. The dessert consists of two deep pink, palm-size macaron shells sandwiching whole red raspberries in a pool of rose and lychee cream. A velvety red rose petal garnishes the whole thing, with a droplet of clear syrup positioned like a dewy jewel on top. And I'm swooning again just thinking about it.

With an impressive number of Pierre Hermé cafés and patisseries in cities across France and around Europe, the United Kingdom, and the Middle East, you may be lucky enough to find an example of the original dessert approved by the inventor himself. But you can have a similar experience at other fine pastry shops; many chefs around the world have been inspired to replicate the Ispahan and to create other cakes, confections, and pink ice creams made with the signature combination of roses, almonds, raspberries, and lychee. A truly good Ispahan is made with the tenderest of macaron shells, smooth and crisp on the outside but moist and chewy in the middle. The dessert should strike you as a subtle feat of edible architecture, with fragile, airy shells holding up the heavier fruit and cream. If you can take a moment to properly luxuriate in this, a cloud of fragrance around your Ispahan might transport you to an imaginary rose garden in summer, at the peak of a long and languorous bloom. I remember the one I savored by a tranquil fountain in the 6th arrondissement as one of the dreamiest dessert experiences of my life.

Kakigori & Bingsu

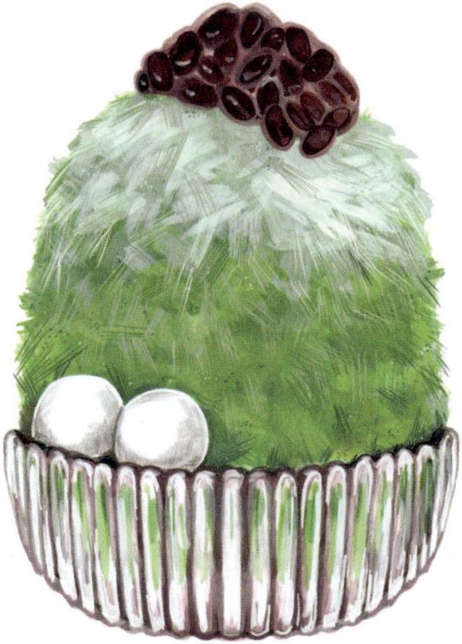

Kakigori with Matcha, Red Bean, and Mochi

I thought I knew what ice was. But it turns out that *shaved* ice is an entirely novel entity. You might think of the gritty convenience store slushies that you drink with a straw from a tall waxy cup, or the denser snow cones that come drenched in bright red or blue syrup. If you are feeling fancy, you might even imagine the crystalline shards of an Italian granita, scented with almond extract and stuffed (miraculously) into a brioche in Sicily. All of these are wonderfully icy things that bring up various joyful summer memories. But none of these coarser, grainy cousins compare to the specific and delicate texture of shaved ice, sheared into the thinnest of white ribbons that just barely cohere before they melt instantly in your warm mouth.

More than a few of the elaborate desserts in this book made me gasp unselfconsciously when I tasted them. Some made me swoon or even well up with tears. But nothing compares to how I felt having taken my first bite of Kakigori, a Japanese-style shaved-ice dessert. Granted, I was already lightheaded and overwhelmed after wandering through dense Tokyo streets on a hot summer day. But a single spoonful of Kakigori made me gasp, swoon, *and* weep. And halfway through this cold, exhilarating treat, buzzing from the matcha caffeine on an empty stomach, it was all I could do not to also burst out laughing. It took all my reserve to not declare to everyone around me at the dessert bar, "I LOVE YOU!" This is the power of Kakigori. Mounded and garnished lavishly, it is an experience of pure giddiness.

On a hot, hot day, it is well worth it to walk past the casual slushies and snow cones in search of a Kakigori. To prepare this treat, a block of ice is typically shaved on the spot for you by hand (or by electric machine) in a sequence of theatrical gestures. It is quickly served in a tall, snowy mound drizzled richly with condensed milk, mochi, fruit, red beans, and/or various artisanal syrups flavored with things like coffee, cherry blossom, or yuzu lemon. Don't be alarmed by how large your serving might be! The whole dessert is so airy and ultrafine that it's light as a heap of fallen snow. I assure you, you will finish

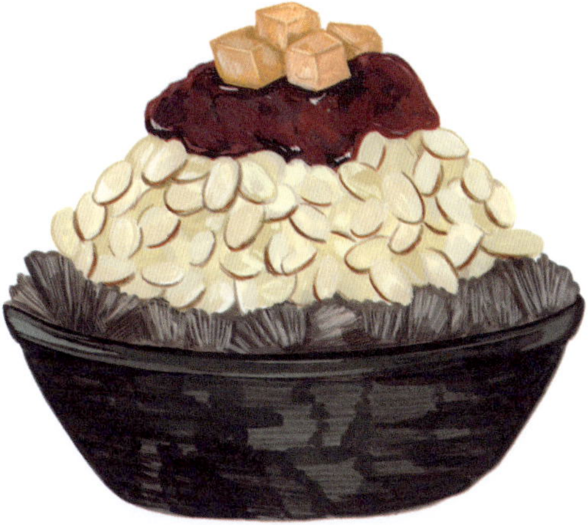

Bingsu with Almonds, Red Bean, Kinako, and Mochi

it—and so quickly and wistfully that, when it's gone, you might wonder if it was all a dream.

Where I live, a true Kakigori is hard to find, but the popular and equally refreshing Korean version of shaved ice, Bingsu, is a reliable city staple. Bingsu is also prepared quickly on site by a server shaving ice into delicate melting wisps, and it also comes in a wonderful variety of flavors. The shops near me in Toronto's Little Korea offer it dotted with fresh strawberries or bananas or gorgeous pourings of savory black sesame cream. My favorite version includes kinako, a peanut-buttery roasted soybean powder that is sprinkled generously all over, with a handful of soft mochi dumplings and silky lashings of condensed milk.

Kashmiri Chai

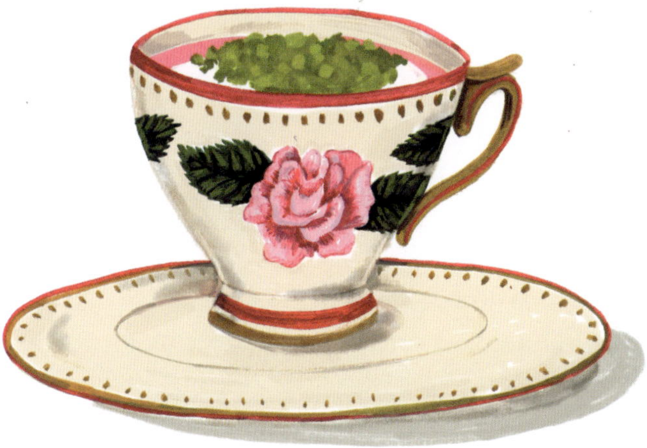

Kashmiri Chai

OK, I know this isn't a dessert. It's a cup of tea. But if you are lucky enough to have a Little India neighborhood or a Pakistani paan shop nearby, you should get in line and order a Kashmiri Chai right this minute. While you wait (for some reason, the tea needs to be conjured in a far back room for a long time before it comes out nuclear-hot), I hope you get to watch a skilled paanwala artfully wrapping fresh green betel leaves around smears of pastes, areca nuts, spices, rose jam, and sprinkles. When your tea order finally arrives, you will receive a cup of thick, caramelized milk in a surprising shade of bright pink.

You might think of it less as a tea beverage than a bowl of boiling ice cream. With a handful of chopped green pistachios garnishing the rosy surface, this is an extravagant and *crunchy* cup of tea. Even in a paper cup, it is as posh and celebratory as the variety shows playing simultaneously on two televisions, with performers dancing in brightly embroidered saris, glittering with sequins.

I've tried many times to reproduce this special form of chai at home. I've simmered green Pakistani tea, star anise, saffron, cardamom, and lots of sugar for over an hour (some recipes suggest three hours!) in milk and cream. I always add the chopped pistachios on top, but I can't quite bring myself to include the red food coloring so often used to make the whole drink so vividly pink. I've never quite replicated the experience of drinking it at my favorite Lahore paan shop, though. There, I like to sip the celebratory dessert-drink surrounded by rainbow-colored garlands. And among so many happy kids, staying up extra-late eating kulfi ice pops and corn on the cob with their parents.

Kunafa & Mahalabiyeh

Kunafa is a sweet and salty Middle Eastern dessert. It's made with a crispy mat of shredded pastry stuffed with a stretchy, melting sheep cheese. The entire thing is soaked in a fragrant, sugary syrup. Sometimes the buttery pastry is golden, sticking out in thin curly tendrils, and the syrup is scented with rose. In other variations, the nest of pastry is tinted a dark orange and set against a pretty, contrasting garnish of chopped green pistachios.

The best Kunafa I've had was in the suburbs of Toronto, where I made a special pilgrimage to taste a Palestinian version made with Nabulsi cheese imported from the West Bank. The shop also offered many other freshly prepared delights. Among those I couldn't resist were an oily sponge cake made with Lotus Biscoff cookie butter (see page 30); slices of sticky walnut baklava; and the lightest of all pastries made with a shattering, featherlight shell of phyllo and overflowing with milky Nutella.

I ordered a tray of cardamom teas and a box of these irresistible sweets to go. While I waited at the bakery under a draped Palestinian flag, passionate protesters on the street outside called for peace and freedom from occupation in Palestine.

I was reminded of the first time I tasted Palestinian food. It was in downtown Pittsburgh, of all places, where I stood in a long line for a takeout restaurant / art installation called Conflict Kitchen. Made by the artists Dawn Weleski, Jon Rubin, and Brett Yasko, Conflict Kitchen was a collaborative contemporary

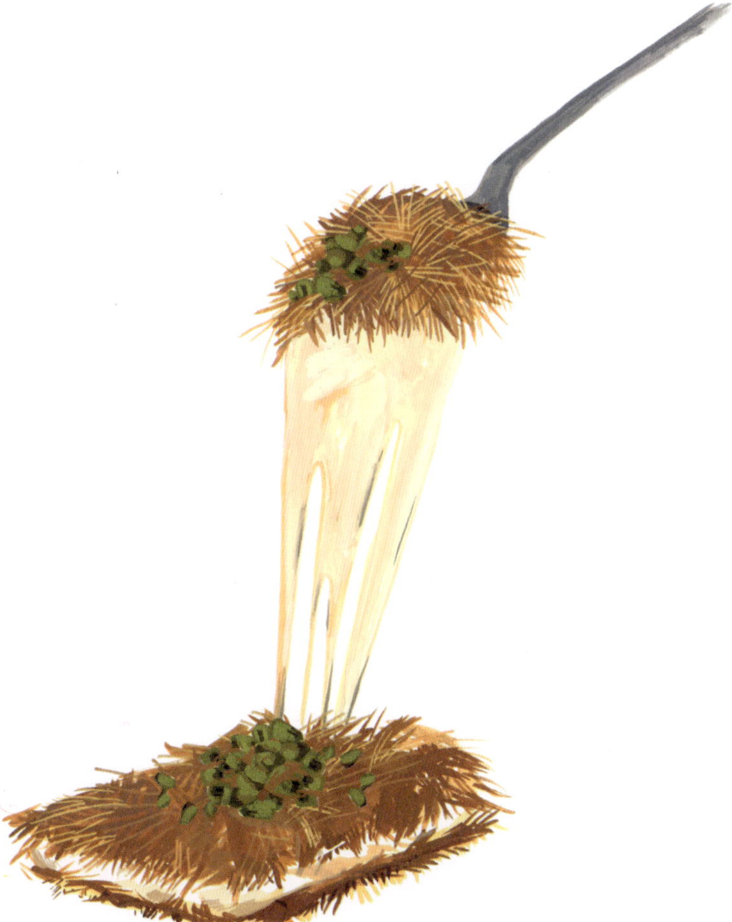

Palestinian Kunafa

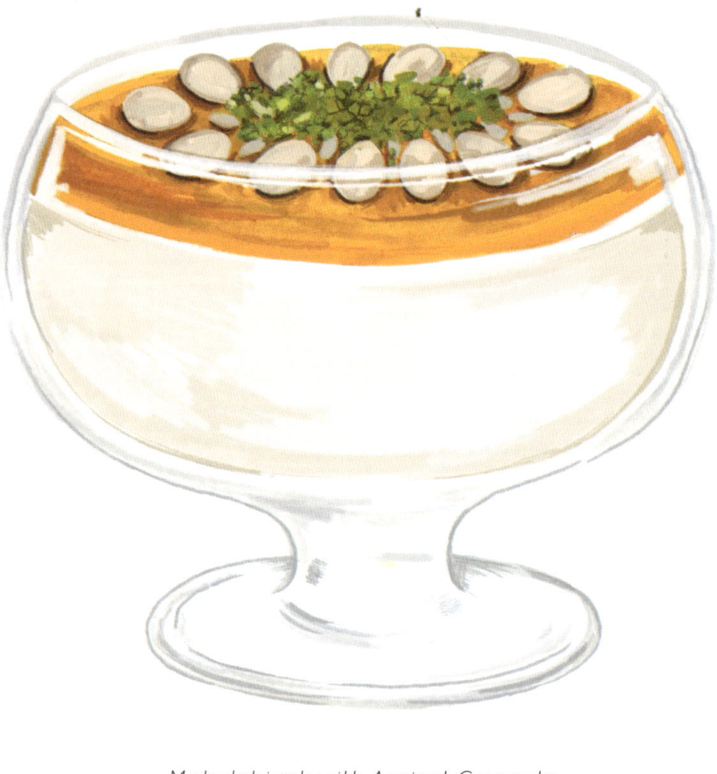

Mahalabiyeh with Apricot Compote

art project that used food and storytelling to share the cultures of people suffering from geopolitical conflict to which the US government contributed.

Over the course of several years, the founders worked with chefs, artists, filmmakers, performers, journalists, and educators from around the world to cook and serve food and to share everyday experiences from Afghanistan, Cuba, Iran, North Korea, and Palestine. When I visited, the restaurant was collaborating with chef Laila El-Haddad to serve a fantastic lunch of baba ghanoush, a spicy tomato and dill salsa called *salata gazawiyya*, various mezze, and more. All this was presented in colorful packaging printed with traditional Arabic design motifs and detailed stories from Palestinians' everyday lives in the United States and under Israeli occupation.

In her cookbook *The Gaza Kitchen*, El-Haddad describes other Palestinian desserts, such as namoura, a semolina and yogurt cake drenched with syrup and sprinkled with pine nuts, and Mahalabiyeh, which I also tasted at Conflict Kitchen. Mahalabiyeh is a delicate milk pudding scented with cardamom and orange blossom water, two of the most heavenly and transporting fragrances.

Visiting Conflict Kitchen was like visiting a Palestinian family kitchen where traditional dishes and personal stories are generously shared. In her book, El-Haddad describes the process of gathering recipes from Palestinian women in Gaza and notes how people were surprised to be asked about their treasured food traditions instead of their experience as victims of conflict. "Of course, it all figures together," she says, "but they were all just extremely delighted that people were thinking about them, and interested in learning about them, as human beings."[5]

*

In the suburbs of Toronto, my family took our box of still-hot Kunafa to the nearby community garden, where my father grows tomatoes, basil, and fava beans. We found a low table and followed the instructions included with our pastry, pouring a cup of clear syrup all over our melting dessert. The sun shone, bees circled drunkenly around us, and we enjoyed a luxuriously sweet picnic, taking turns pinching our fingers into the warm mozzarella-like cheese in a pool of errant pastry threads. Everything was shiny from all the oil and syrup, and our hands and arms were sticky up to our elbows. My son drank the strong tea, charged up to the max with sugar, and looked nervously at me to see if I was going to stop him. I didn't. Other community gardeners from our sprawling diasporic city came by and leaned in convivially to share.

Food makes our stories tangible and brings us together. My experience with Kunafa was a small reminder of the belonging and joy that are possible across differences, in a just and peaceful world that everyone deserves.

Lemon Lavender Shortbread

I've mostly kept cookies out of this book, since the vast realm of biscuity things—studded with chocolate chips, crafted into tidy sandwiches, or dipped expediently into one's breakfast coffee—would fill a dedicated volume of its own.

But this guideline became irrelevant in the wake of a square of Lemon Lavender Shortbread I found displayed under a glass cloche at a neighborhood bakery in a small American town. It was deep and moist, and frosted with a thin layer of zippy, lemony icing. Anyone would be forgiven for describing this less as a cookie and more as the butteriest-ever kind of cake.

Shortbread is iconic. Three cheers for the medieval Scots who invented it, and for the generations of Scottish bakers who perfected this specific kind of thick-cut, *heavy* shortbread. You know, the kind that is so rich you need to eat it in thin translucent slivers, slowly, and with a fork? And gratitude to the English who garnished and amended shortbread with fruit and blossoms—like the piece I ate, which was adorned with bright yellow lemon zest and elevated by lavender, that perfumy prince among heady edible flowers.

Hear me when I declare my love for every form of shortbread! I crave biscuits with crunchy crystals of sugar all over, broken into rectangles and soaked to the collapsing point in a cup of milky tea. During the holidays, I lunge toward the ubiquitous pale circles of shortbread studded with chewy little maraschino cherries, so fine-grained and soft that they melt into powdery

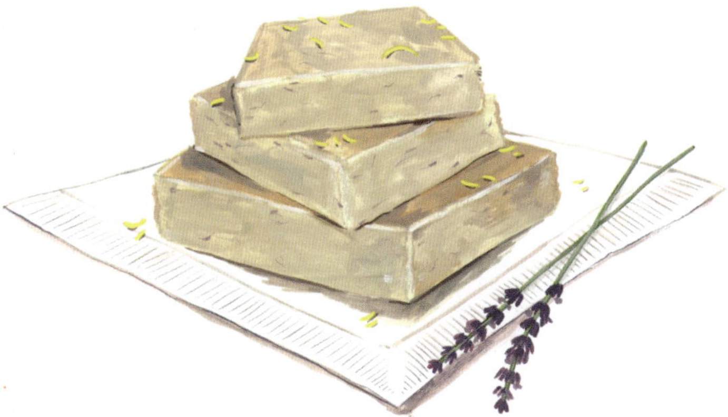

Lemon Lavender Shortbread

cashmere in my mouth. I'll take any flavor—sweet or savory, from chocolate to thyme or even spruce needles—kneaded into a buttery base or sprinkled on top as a beckoning garnish. Join me in tasting every delicious variation of shortbread. It is one of the simplest and greatest achievements of dessert culture.

At least once, though, I invite you to summon a picture of dainty tea parties, Elizabethan petticoats, and royal weddings, and order the Lemon Lavender Shortbread. If these images make you cringe so much that you want to throw a pretty hat into a ravine, I feel you. Throw the pretty hat! Stomp your boots! Pierce your nose and dye your hair an impolite shade at once! Without apology or restraint, the most punk thing to do, I think, would be to love some outrageously perfect shortbread anyway. Think of it as a pound of butter with sunshine mixed into it.

MANGO POMELO SAGO

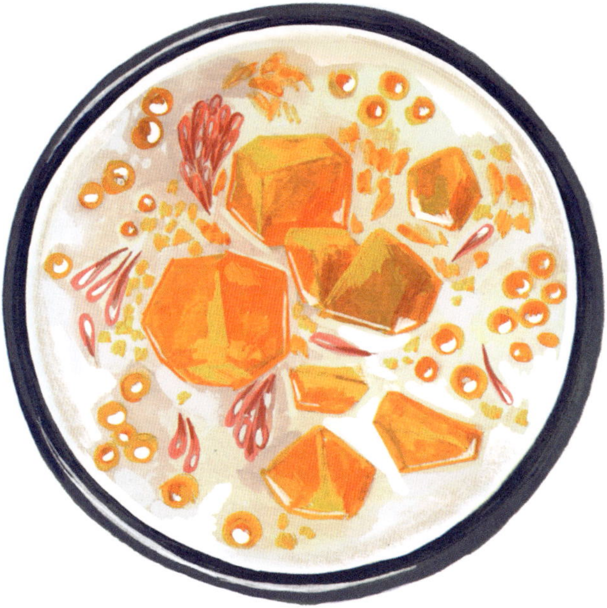

Jumbo Mango Pomelo Sago

Among high-rise buildings, strip malls, and a densely packed transportation hub in the biggest suburb of Toronto, you can find one of the most diverse concentrations of immigrants. You can visit restaurants serving global specialities in English, Urdu, Arabic, Mandarin, Polish, Punjabi, Tagalog, Portuguese, Spanish, Cantonese, Hindi, Vietnamese, and Tamil, among so many more languages.

It is in this international context that I meet my Italian Canadian mother at a bright café, directly in sight of her apartment window, that serves her favorite Hong Kong Chinese desserts. She isn't the only one completely obsessed with the desserts in this restaurant. Now that I too have tasted a Mango Pomelo Sago, I understand and would describe *both* of us this way. We are evangelical in our enthusiasm about this dessert. I order one every single time I visit now, thinking about it distractedly before family dinner, and during dinner, and after. I have, on occasion, made the long drive to the suburbs *not* to visit my parents (please don't tell them) but just to shut my eyes and wrap my mouth around a spoonful of this soupy nirvana; this pure, cooling, mango pool of heavenly bliss; this dessert whose voluptuous mouthful of a name is worthy of poetry and song: Mango Pomelo Sago.

Mango Pomelo Sago was first popularized at a restaurant chain in Singapore and then in Hong Kong, but you can now find your own bowl in big cities and suburbs where Hong Kong desserts, bubble teas, and dim sum are sold. If you can order a "jumbo," I recommend it. Don't be alarmed by the scale of what looks like a giant's champagne goblet filled to overflowing with chunks of ripe mango, house-made mango ice cream, and mango pudding, plus slippery sago pearls and hidden gifts of chewy, marble-size mochi. Shards of juicy pink pomelo are mounded together with everything in a gorgeous heap, all of it swimming in a pool of silky coconut milk. Every natural flavor and sensuous texture is in perfect proportion; not one bite of it is cloying. Don't be tricked into sharing it! I can assure you, you will eat every last drop, and it will be difficult to do so without the kinds of audible exclamations of pleasure one does not usually make in front of one's mother.

Mango Pomelo Sago is especially crave-worthy and refreshing if it's hot and humid outside and you are thirsty or tired. To all these things, it is the antidote. However, I recommend getting it in any weather, even in the darkest depths of sleeting winter. A few sips might prompt dreams that you are not in a strip mall in the suburbs in the dirty snow, but under a coconut tree. Warm. Among mango trees and blooming tropical flowers . . .

MAPLE SYRUP PIE

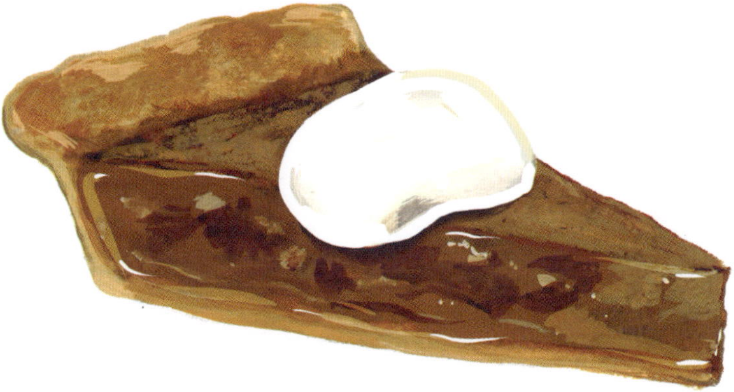

Maple Syrup Pie

"The thing that is magical about maple syrup," my friend Shannon tells me, "is how much it's influenced by the environment in any given year." Shannon is an artist and small-scale maple syrup producer. "The soil, the weather, temperature changes, the microbial activity taking place in each tree . . . it all affects the flavor and color of your batch. The term *terroir* must have been invented for it."

Shannon should know all about this magic. At her snowy farm in eastern Ontario, I've seen her poring over a wood fire, keeping its energy hot and alive every day for several weeks at the end of winter, just when the temperatures oscillate between above freezing during the day and below freezing at night. She stirs her steaming pans of sap, which she has collected from a few dozen trees strung all over with hoses like garlands. Under the sugaring moon, she checks each tree for signals to guide the process. Are the buds breaking? Did the sap change color or turn skunky? Is she taking too much? What do the anxious squirrels think about it all?

Still using technologies developed by Indigenous peoples over thousands of years, Shannon is part of a long history of producers, large and small, who have harvested the thin, watery sap of sugar maple trees and celebrated the first precious food of early spring after the hunger gap of winter. Shannon performs the long hard work of evaporating the sap down from a water-to-sugar ratio of 40 to 1 over a hand-built fire. But most producers make this delicious and iconic regional ingredient in giant industrial evaporators. The scale of this project—ranging across the hardwood forests in southern Ontario, Quebec, and the Maritimes in Canada and into the midwestern United States—is fortunate for the world, which hungers for millions of gallons of sweet, resinous maple syrup and crystalized sugar every year.

To really taste the forest in an ideal state, I would recommend you put on your hooded parka, trudge through some muddy, melting snow, and join a traditional maple syrup maker by the fire. The sky should be blue and the air cold and fresh. Dip a sticky mug into a steel pan of sweetening, smoky, boiling sap and drink this maple magic up. Drink it straight!

I confess, even as a Canadian, I've only ever caught a moment as sweet and iconic as this a few times in my life. Every March and April, though, I can find the second-best thing. If you don't have a creative friend in the sugar bush, find yourself a generous serving of syrup in the form of a complete dessert, namely Maple Syrup Pie.

Say no to distracting pecans and raisins, and even to ice cream as a garnish. Focus on the delicate natural maple flavor and fragrance of the precious ingredients. Only a little unsweetened whipped cream—you really don't need to add any more sugar—can complement such a pie.

There are strong opinions in Canada on the matter of the best tarts and who invented them, but let me suggest you look for a bakery selling what's called a *sugar pie*, or *tarte au sucre*, in the Quebecois style: all soft, opaque, and jammy in the middle, as the maple syrup is baked together with eggs and cream. Or seek out my personal favorite, the Ontario butter-tart style of Maple Syrup Pie, where glossy, runny syrup is sealed under a thin caramelized skin until you bite into it. Do your own research. If it's really good, delicious maple syrup will spill out all over your chin and onto the front of your shirt.

Matcha Parfait & Flower Parfait

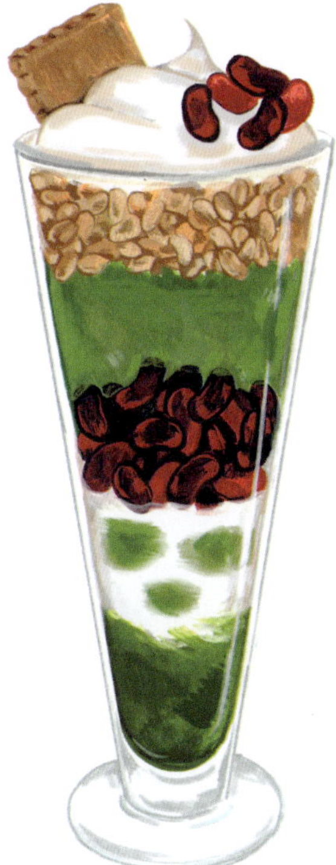

Tokyo Matcha Parfait

A Matcha Parfait is essentially a grown-up sundae. Everywhere I went to try one, I found only elegantly dressed adults enjoying them, sometimes with their eyes closed in a mature sort of quiet reverence. I performed most of my parfait tasting in Tokyo, where these desserts are especially popular and have been fashioned into a form of high culture. There is something decidedly theatrical about their presentation. They are served in a tall, stemmed, vase-shaped glass to show the various contrasting strata of colors, creams, fruit, dumplings, and crispy things. When a Matcha Parfait is carried to your table, it draws envy from all the other patrons, who might wish they had splurged on such a showy, expensive dessert for themselves.

The most memorable parfait I tasted (and I dutifully sampled quite a few) was at the Ginza location of the venerable old tea store chain Nakamura Tokichi, renowned for green teas and desserts. It's not unusual to wait in line for hours to get in to taste a parfait or to drink a thick, frothy cup of whisked matcha at this elegantly appointed café. Their wonderful matcha, like all real Japanese matcha, is made with the finest handpicked, shade-grown tea leaves, steamed, dried, and ground into a powder. The good stuff is very fresh, tastes a little bitter and a little marine, and leaves a faintly sweet taste on the palate. Try to imagine essences of the darkest chocolate, coldest oysters, and freshest sweet peas all stirred together; this is what good matcha tastes like.

My own Matcha Parfait came with an illustrated card describing the anatomy of the seasonal dessert. The card detailed every ingredient in order, beginning at the top with pale green matcha whipped cream sprinkled with matcha powder, cooling matcha ice cream, fluffy matcha chiffon cake, two fresh raspberries, and one roasted chestnut. Nestled among these layers were small, chewy shiratama dango rice dumplings. Then came a layer of

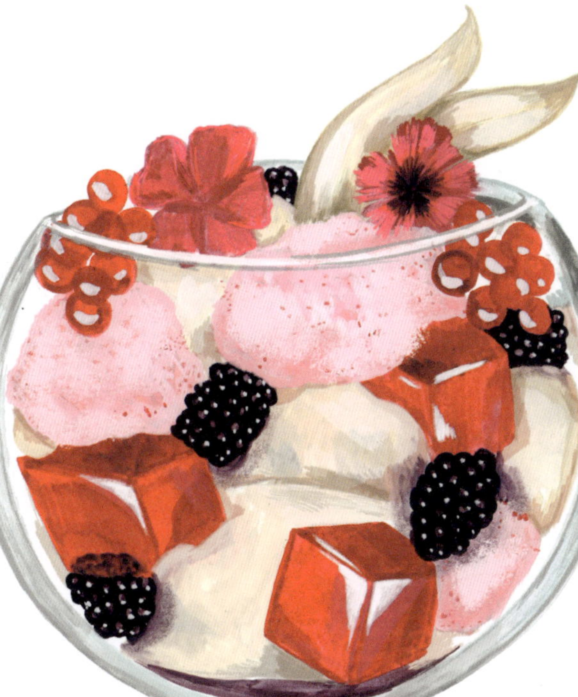

Rose, Flower, and Fruit Parfait

crispy puffed millet, some jiggly matcha tea jelly, the darkest green matcha bean paste, crunchy red beans for color and contrasting texture, a little creamy vanilla soft serve, and finally, resting at the bottom of the glass in a dainty pool, the koicha—a dense sauce of barely moistened, pure green matcha. My parfait had enough caffeine in one spoonful to make a woman levitate, as if I weren't on the ceiling already, coursing with buzzy bliss just *thinking* about all this matcha happiness.

While I paced myself through the bitter tea and the sweetened creams, chewy dumplings, and puffs of grain, I chatted with a nearby family from Holland who were also making their way through their own inverse matcha mountains. We narrated our own parfaits as we went through them, marveling together at the creativity and care taken in Japanese confectionery arts. The woman told me that she and her family always travel this way. "We arrive in a city," she said, "and go from cake, to cake, to cake!"

In the spirit of gastronomic adventure, they recommended another memorable parfait, which I would later taste at a flower-shop café, where not only was I surrounded by greenery, but there were frilly pink roses bursting out from holes in the modified terrarium-like tabletops.

My Flower Parfait came in a palm-size glass orb showing the extravagantly pretty layers in what I came to think of as an edible flower garden. Foamy mousse and cubes of cake, ice cream, red currants, custardy cheesecake, crispy cereals, and quivering, pink rose-scented jelly were all bound attractively together and topped with rose petals. It was full of light and lightness; it was the food of angels. And, inevitably, the food of Instagram. While I relished mine in dainty spoonfuls, feeling purified and absolved of all sins, the woman next to me spent a surprising amount of time staging and documenting herself in selfies beside the Flower Parfait. It was as if the dessert were too beautiful to eat, and she was made prettier just by her proximity to it.

While it might be called a *sundae*, a *trifle*, or even a *beaker cake*, you will know an elegant, grown-up parfait when you see one. If you can, order it in a comfortable dessert café where an infinite number of possible cakes, creams, crisps, fruits, flowers, and matcha are composed and contrasted in a tall glass. If you need to document your gastronomic trophy, do it quickly and get your distracting device out of sight. Then enjoy your elegant dessert with the sense you are on a journey through a succession of stimulating, surprising, and emotional experiences. Closing your eyes to focus on the contrasting sensations would be a perfectly understandable thing to do.

Medovik

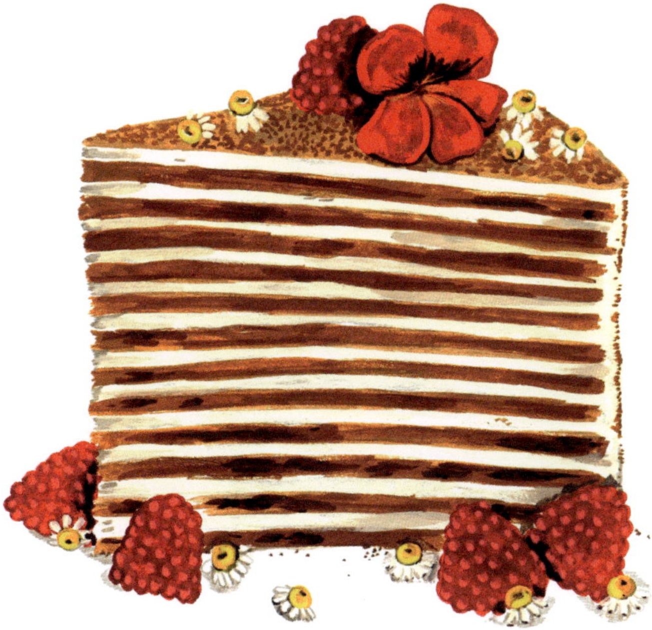

Medovik

It's hard for me to evaluate this dessert objectively, because I ate my first slice of Medovik on the same day I saw a total eclipse of the sun. I don't know if I was still vibrating from the days' worth of anticipation and the delivery of a celestial spectacle in a wide blue sky that no weather forecaster had anticipated, or if I was just terribly hungry from the long drive back to the city. When a slice of this golden cake landed on my plate, the emotional release I had hoped for but failed to feel under the sun's shimmery corona surged up all at once. One bite of it filled my eyes with tears.

A wide variety of delicious honey cakes are made across cultures around the world. Medovik is made with thirteen or fourteen layers of thin sponge and generous slathers of sweetened sour cream, all flavored with honey burnt to the edge of incandescence. This one is most often associated with Ukraine and Russia, though it is also beloved throughout all the countries of the former Soviet Union.

Search your own city for a Ukrainian bakery or Russian tearoom where you might find a good Medovik. I wish you a tall, elegant slice, with some hot black tea from the samovar poured into a gilded porcelain cup.

If you cannot find a purveyor, you may need to appeal to your most ambitious baking friend and convince them to make one for you. Do whatever it takes! Help them clear two or three days in their calendar to get this right. They'll need to paint cookie sheet after cookie sheet with thin batter and heat honey to a state of caramelization nail-bitingly close to scorching.

In the meantime, prepare your palate for this extravagant gift. Read about the honeybees, those other essential collaborators in this gastronomic spectacle. Find out just how many thousands of flowers one worker bee would need to visit to make a single spoonful of honey before she expires after gathering so much nectar. Like me, you might get a little weepy and let loose some tears of relief and awe and gratitude for sunlight and fragrant flowers, for all the creatures and their preciousness, for the existence of cake, and for so much beauty in the world.

Mille-Feuilles

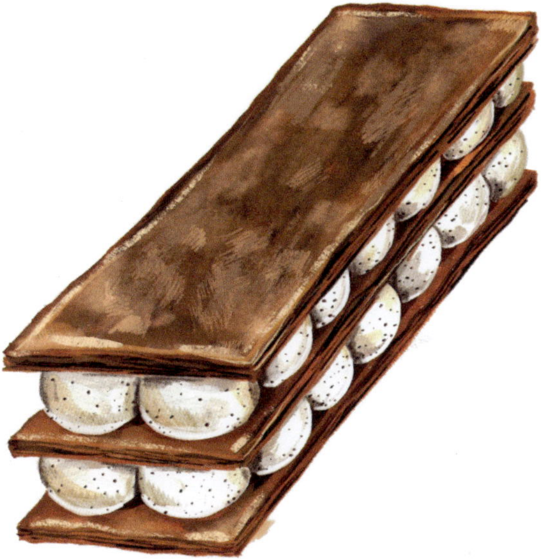

Vanilla Mille-Feuille

The traditional French version of Mille-Feuilles is made with rectangles of ultra-crisp caramelized pastry layered with stiff dollops of cream and, sometimes, ground nuts and fruit. Many Americans would call something like this a *napoleon*, a dessert that typically includes a heavier custard between the pastry layers and is topped with a white royal icing, styled with signature wavy chocolate stripes. Whatever you call it, a Mille-Feuille is a delicious and regal invention. When you find an enticing one, be sure it is assembled especially for you at the very last moment. Do this to feel as important as the emperor of France (without having to be as cruel) and also to ensure your pastry will be crisp for as long as it takes to devour it.

My favorite source of Mille-Feuilles in my own neighborhood—a Japanese-owned French-style patisserie—keeps one single sample in the display case among their other confections. A little sign next to it reassures hungry customers (who might want two?): "Don't worry, we will make it for you!" I know that this extra service is an act of thoughtfulness and care, both for the experience of customers and for the specific integrity of crisp pastry. This is part of what makes me want one. And the more I think about it, I want one immediately!

The specific architecture of a Mille-Feuille, with scaffolding made of crisp pastry and cream, is an ideal frame for all sorts of memorable flavors and inventive combinations of ingredients. Many summers ago, in a pastry case in France, I saw one that I have never forgotten: blazingly caramelized, sticky and blistered, full of saffron-flavored cream layered with peach compote and wisps of *edible gold*. I regret not communing more closely with that otherworldly pastry when I had the chance. But I am still confirmed in my belief that a well-made, plain vanilla Mille-Feuilles are already a sublime thing. And I have known many, made even more dazzling with the modest (and wise) addition of a few fresh raspberries between the layers.

Recently, I was happy to read in my door-stopping *Penguin Companion to Food* not only that *mille feuilles* translates to "a thousand leaves" but also that "since one sheet of puff pastry, conventionally made, comprises 729 laminations, and mille feuilles may have two to five layers (1,458 to 3,645 leaves) . . . *this is an accurate description*."[6] So it's not just a metaphor; a Mille-Feuille literally does have thousands of layers! I know I am going to recount this little-known fact again and again (maybe even memorizing the math to do it justice) whenever I invite my friends to join me in eating one. With our full and informed appreciation, we can only enjoy more the blissful shattering of each and every layer as it yields between our teeth.

MOCHI DONUTS

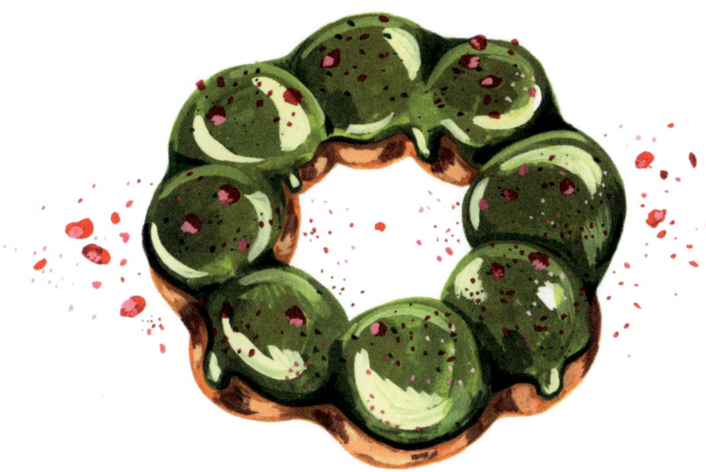

Matcha and Rose Mochi Donut

Creative innovations abound in donut fashion, and it was difficult for me to choose just one or two great examples for this volume. One booming trend worth alerting dessert-o-philes to is the Mochi Donut, a chewy, bulbous confection in the shape of a teething ring—or maybe a sex toy, depending on how you look at it.

The first fried Mochi Donuts were available in Hawaii. Then Mister Donut, a Japanese chain, joined eight gumball-size pieces of dough into the treat we recognize today, and its popularity soared. Made with mochiko (a sweet Japanese rice flour also used to make mochi), along with starchy taro or gummy tapioca flour, Mochi Donuts offer a unique and varied textural experience. The tantalizing deep-fried crown is dark and chewy at the narrow joints, while the center of each golden ball holds warm, stretchy, spongy mochi batter that flirts with being just a little undercooked in the middle.

The donuts are often decorated with a colorful glaze and flecked with any number of textural enhancements, from Pocky sticks to zingy bits of dehydrated berries. The plain, lightly sweetened donut base might be dressed up to taste like Vietnamese coffee, Hokkaido milk tea (topped with boba, of course), banana milk, or Hawaiian Kona mud pie. Or your donut might come in some other complex flavor combination, like Thai mango sticky rice, chewy Korean injeolmi cake, cinnamony churro, or even the garishly bright and chemical Fruity Pebbles cereal. The possibilities are so varied, and so international, that you could almost explore all of global dessert culture in one place as it's piped and piled onto Mochi Donuts!

You could order only one. Or you could bring home a kaleidoscopic dozen and share the splendor with all your hungry friends.

MONT BLANC

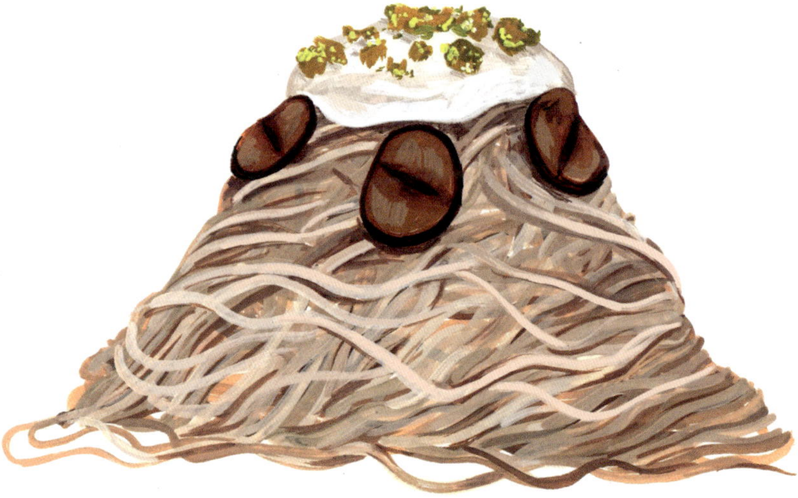

Chestnut Mont Blanc

Oh, to experience this dessert for the first time again! It wasn't in Northern Italy, where its namesake mountain is located; nor in Paris, where the dessert was invented; nor in the fall, when its signature ingredient (the bursting, porcupine-like chestnut) is harvested. I tasted a Mont Blanc for the first time in the spring, in Kyoto, at a ritzy café by the banks of the Kamo River, among blossoming dogwood trees. There, trying hard not to be distracted with concern about my credit card limit, I lifted elegant spoonfuls of this dessert from a wide plate that was cracked and weathered in just the right places and dotted with flakes of gold.

To make Mont Blanc, the starchy, lightly sweetened meat of a chestnut is cooked and pureed into a dense, creamy paste. In Japan, my server demonstrated the assembly of the dessert. First, she pressed a tennis ball–size handful of chestnut paste through a tall extruding machine embedded in a grand, rustic wood frame. Then, in a graceful, practiced performance, she swirled the spagettini-thin, fragile chestnut noodles around and around over a base of weightless meringue, cake, and whipped cream. By the time I was presented with my very own swirling mountain of noodley lightness, I was fully hypnotized.

With its hilly shape and snowy cap of even more cream, the dessert was inspired by one of the tallest mountains in Europe, the Mont Blanc (or White Mountain), which straddles the French and Italian border. I wonder, regardless of when or where you experience it: Is this dessert supposed to give you a view into another world?

I may never be able to afford to go to the Mont Blanc café again for this dessert, which was the most expensive treat I've ever tasted. I ate it reverently, down to the last wisp of gold leaf, instead of lunch. But luckily, we can all probably find a modest version of a classic Mont Blanc in French bakeries and other stylish urban cafés. The chestnut paste will be swirled onto a meringue or a cream-filled shortbread crust, or perhaps presented as a chestnut mousse and cake. We might even find chestnuts replaced with other subtly flavored, starchy autumn ingredients—like squash or the vivid purple taro potato. I noticed incredible color-saturated purple Mont Blancs all over Japan! Whatever the flavor, you'll know it's a Mont Blanc in spirit when some core of treasure is swathed in a loose pile of delicately flavored noodles. Enjoy the way it expands your perspective while it melts in your mouth.

MOONCAKE

You will know it is mid-autumn when the fall chrysanthemums begin to droop, the nights get longer and colder, and Mooncakes are suddenly ubiquitous in supermarkets, bakeries, and tea shops with a big Chinese diasporic clientele. The most common version of the palm-size filled pastry is luxurious and weighty. Ornate molds are used to shape Mooncakes into tidy geometric forms or jaunty animals, like piglets, rabbits, or Japanese lucky waving cats. With a smooth pastry made (most often) with vegetable oil or lard and burnished in the oven, the whole treat can look and feel like a shiny puck of gold.

Mooncakes are often stamped with decorative motifs, like flowers; Cantonese symbols wishing luck, harmony, and longevity; intersecting woven lines and vines; and sometimes the name and logo of the shop selling them. Popular shops have even begun to mass-produce them in bright colors and offer them in honor of the moon during the Mid-Autumn Festival or the Lunar New Year.

While prepackaged Mooncakes are sweet, filling, and economical, look for the freshly made variety from a good Chinese bakery during the fall when they are in season. I love the sweet and savory salted duck egg yolk version, with a bright orange orb (representing the full moon) glowing in a bed of tan lotus seed paste. Traditional Chinese regional styles might be densely filled with red bean paste, a combination of seeds and nuts, or roasted pork. The most contemporary (and controversial)

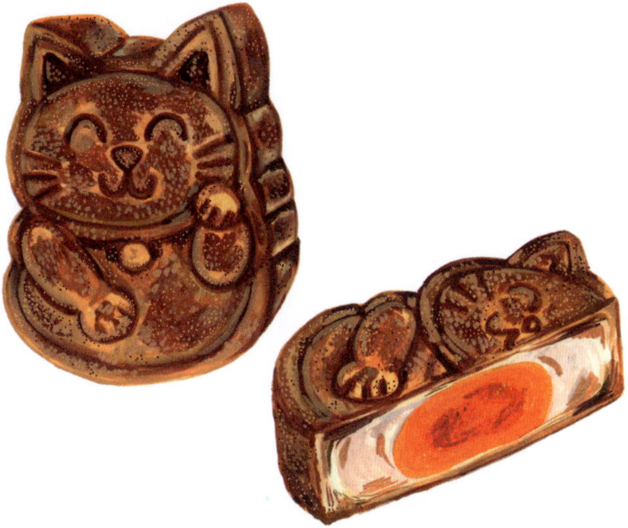

Mooncake with Salted Duck Egg

varieties might contain mochi, lime cream cheese, salted caramel, Earl Grey tea, or even the Italian espresso-based dessert Tiramisu!

Mooncakes are best when sliced with a sharp knife into small, tidy wedges and shared. A small cup of hot green, black, or oolong tea would be the most appropriate and satisfying accompaniment to wash down the sticky, heavy pastry and filling. Another essential ritual would be to make a grateful toast in honor of the big, bright autumn *dessert* moon.

Pavlova
&
Lamingtons

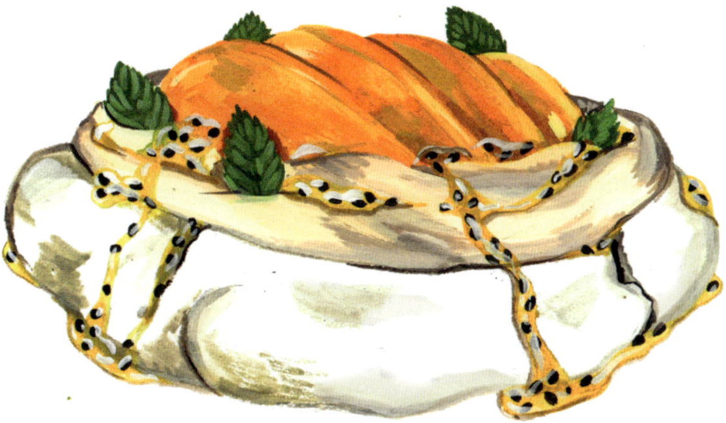

Mango and Passionfruit Pavlova

A Pavlova is a classic dessert made by filling a nest of airy meringue with whipped cream and a mess of syrupy fruit. It was named for the prima ballerina Anna Pavlova, who was famous for her long and storied career, her love of animals (she even kept her own swans!), and her prominently arched feet.

To gain some insight as to why Pavlova (the ballerina) would inspire a meringue dessert, I watched some rare footage of her dancing her famous solo rendition of *The Dying Swan*, choreographed by Mikhail Fokine, in 1905. She is striking in her stiffness and fragility, floating back and forth across the stage in the teeniest, tiniest steps en pointe. She melts backward gracefully with a bendy spine, her movements growing weaker as the piece goes on. Finally, this fairy-woman-swan releases her body to the deathly pull of gravity and folds herself into a fluffy, tutu-shaped heap.

Because of the inspiring ballerina, I had always assumed that the Pavlova was a Russian treat, but it turns out that this assumption is not at all correct. While the exact place of origin of the Pavlova is a matter of great debate, it was actually invented in either New Zealand or Australia in the 1920s, when the ballerina was in the region performing a grand tour. A local chef is said to have been inspired to create a composition as light and ethereal as she was. While I'm pretty convinced New Zealand gets the credit for this one (apologies to Australia), I suggest you do some primary research yourself by searching the dessert menu at a fancy restaurant for a good Pavlova to plunge a spoon into. You will still be uncertain where the Pavlova came from, but you will be so distracted and delighted that origins will probably cease to matter.

Everyone likes berries on a Pavlova, but mangoes and passion fruit (both grown in the New Zealand region) are also common toppings. Pavlovas are especially wonderful with seedy, syrupy tendrils of passion fruit pulp oozing all over the cream and its crackling pillow of meringue. A good Pavlova is a gorgeous

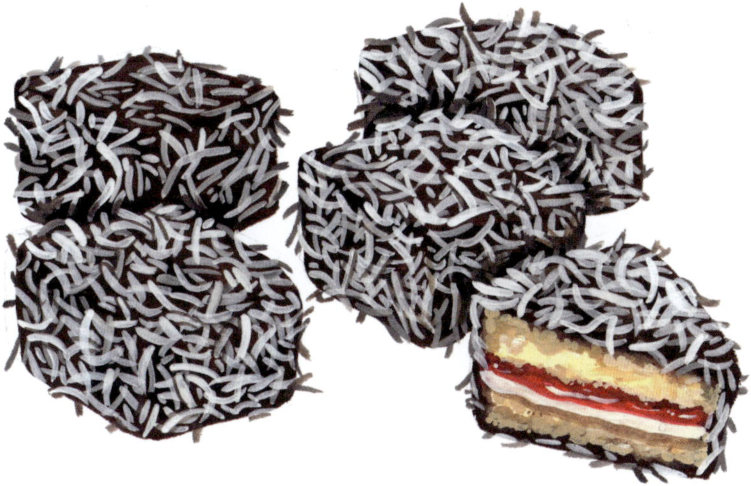

Lamingtons with Raspberry Jam

dessert that barely holds itself together. In a performance of softness, cream, and delicate crunch, it seems about to collapse, gracefully, right into your lap.

If you want to start another row between New Zealanders and Australians, just try and tell the story of the Lamington. (Apologies to New Zealand now, but these were almost definitely invented in Australia.) To make these treats, which are considerably less grand and romantic than a Pavlova, soft cubes of yellow sponge cake are bisected with jam or cream, then dipped into a chocolate glaze and rolled in shredded coconut. A Lamington is an admirable dessert unit, moist and bite-size and perfectly enjoyable beside a cup of coffee or tea.

While Lamingtons are reported to be popular across Eastern Europe, South Africa, and the United States, they are apparently less loved than ever in the region of their invention. In her book *Cake: A Global History*, Nicola Humble writes that a new generation of Australians and New Zealanders are not too impressed by Lamingtons. No matter how delicious they are, they are associated with British culture at a time when the young increasingly prefer East Asian influences. "For them," she writes, "these cakes exist as objects of kitsch—relics from a past receding rapidly out of sight, rather than something they might actually eat."[7] Curiously, Humble reports that their namesake—the Baron Lamington, who served as governor of Queensland in the early 20th century—also hated the cakes and referred to them as "those bloody poofy woolly biscuits."

The first time I tried a Lamington was in a Brooklyn café. A mound of them sat next to the checkout, looking as cute and irresistible as a basket of puppies. Fortunately for tea and cake lovers, even of the English old lady variety, you will find Lamingtons anywhere there is a concentration of Australasians. Sometimes they might even appear in fashionable urban bakeries selling organic sourdough and healthy treats. I can attest that among hipsters in New York, for the time being at least, Lamingtons are welcome and adored.

Pineapple Chamoyada

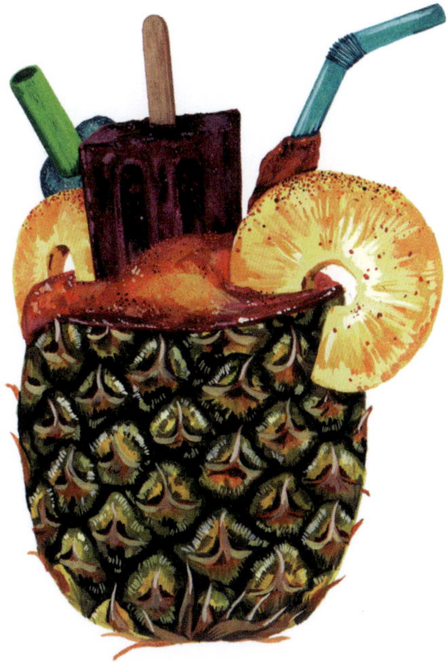

Pineapple Chamoyada

To mark the last day of school—and the beginning of an already scorching, humid summer—I brought my kid to a new Mexican treat shop a short walk from our home. A patient server described all the forms and ingredients of each dessert beyond our favorite sugar-crusted churros. My son was intrigued by the marquesita, a tightly rolled crepe filled with caramel and condensed milk and topped with shredded Edam cheese, which he ate with speed and enthusiasm, if not a sharing spirit.

Seeking something celebratory and thirst-quenching, I ordered the most ambitious, enormous thing on the menu, a Pineapple Chamoyada.

A Chamoyada, in general, is a refreshing mango or pineapple slush topped with tajín, a salty, spicy, sour chili powder condiment made with dried lime zest; hibiscus flowers; and a vinegary brine used to pickle apricots. In the summertime, you might find a Chamoyada at a Mexican restaurant or a stand selling Mexican street food. It can be served simply in a clear plastic cup allowing a view of the sunset-orange slush streaked with syrupy red clouds. Or, if you are as lucky as I was that hot day, it might be a big, flamboyant spectacle of a thing stuffed into a whole pineapple, featuring many of the signature flavors of Mexican gastronomy. The large, icy concoction I ordered was a picture of glorious excess, garnished with pineapple rings, a house-made cucumber ice pop, crunchy roasted peanuts, and even *gummy worms*—all swimming playfully under a coating of brazenly viscous, bright red sauce. It was so tart and eye-wateringly spicy that when it landed on the table in front of me, I involuntarily sent an arc of saliva across the room.

I have since seen Chamoyadas that come festooned with other tropical fruit, watermelon, strawberries, cinnamon horchata popsicles, or even a peeled "bloody mango" on a stick, the fruit dusted all over with fiery spice. Such a wild and refreshing dessert beckons to both the brave and the lavish.

PLANT-BASED CHEESECAKE

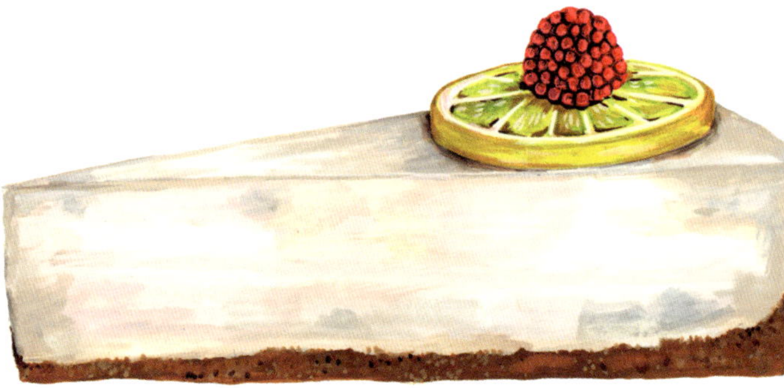

Vegan Lemon Plant-Based Cheesecake

Cafés, bakeries, and ice cream shops that use strictly plant-based ingredients are getting very common in cosmopolitan cities. They are often so good at making pretty, delicious desserts that I sometimes become a regular before I even realize the offerings are vegan! Even this dessert-o-phile and proud butter lover can admit that vegan treats can be delectable when made with nuts, creamy coconut, dates, maple syrup, and other high-quality, flavorful, and healthful ingredients. As long as it's not made from a soulless brick of tofu, Plant-Based Cheesecake can be one of the greats. My favorite is made with finely ground and whipped cashew butter and rich coconut oils. When served cold, this makes for a densely rich and sturdy slice, a suitable palette for fresh fruit decorations and modern, stylish garnishes.

Don't be discouraged by the banner names for this dessert, which might sound blandly vegetal (Plant-Based Cheesecake), morally sanctimonious (vegan cheesecake), tied to faddish weight-loss culture (keto cheesecake), or unappetizingly medical (allergen-free or nondairy cheesecake). Remember, just like your favorite old-fashioned milky cheesecakes, these are flavored with whatever you might be craving, from dark chocolate, coffee, or cardamom to pumpkin spice or yuzu lemon.

Go ahead and seek out a plate of this rich dessert at a sunny table in a street-side café where you can eat thin forkfuls of it under an unruly web of climbing green plants. Feel the extra buzz of goodness that comes from eating something approved by people who are healthier and more virtuous.

Rainbow Cake

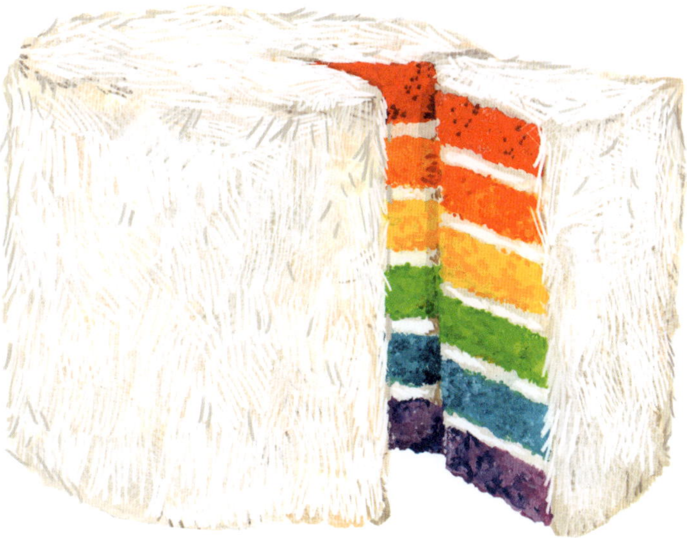

Rainbow Cake with Coconut

Trans and nonbinary food scholar Sasha DuBose defines truly queer food as "taking how we define food and how we engage with it, and twisting it, making it more *fun*."[8] Some of the more over-the-top desserts in this book could fit that description, like the Pineapple Chamoyada. And the water-flavored, nearly invisible Raindrop Cake (see page 164) could certainly be considered queer, as it's a food that goes against mainstream norms of cuisine. But there is one dessert, the Rainbow Cake, that is worth highlighting here because it's both fun and unconventional, and because it's made to nourish and advocate for queer people and communities.

Yes, a Rainbow Cake looks like it belongs at a kid's birthday party and is hardly a gourmand's picture of refinement! And politically, it's fair to wonder whether a crayon-colored symbol could ever really convey the wide spectrum of gender and sexuality. Some might also point out that the rainbow flag's declarations of peace, hope, and the beauty of diversity have been commercialized since its origins in the United States in the 1960s and '70s. So why waste time and money on a cartoon cake? With these valid questions in mind, we should remember that around the world today, rainbow imagery is still sometimes seen as dangerous and controversial. Like books and flags and expressions of love in public, a brightly colored slice of Rainbow Cake could even be forcibly *banned.*

If you can enjoy a celebratory Pride event in your favorite city (or invent one), then that day is not a day to eat something sensible. You and I both know exactly how this multilayered extravaganza is going to taste: sweet as candy and regrettable as a plate of vegetable shortening. There is so much food coloring saturating every layer of a Rainbow Cake that there is a good chance that eating one will also give you a headache. Eat a large and brilliant slice anyway. Because this is still a radical and necessary cake.

Order the kind with cream cheese icing or a little coconut all over if you can find it. Wash it down with a plastic cup of beer. Gorge on a slice of Rainbow Cake by yourself, or split it with someone you love, because you *can*. Feel good about supporting independent queer bakers and bakeries that demonstrate solidarity with their LGBTQ+ communities. Order the Rainbow Cake because you are in a city that welcomes a celebration of the basic human right to love and to enjoy one's own body, both in private and in the middle of the street.

Dare to taste it all and have no regrets. To all the fun, over-the-top, fabulous food lovers everywhere, happy Pride.

RAINDROP CAKE & ANMITSU

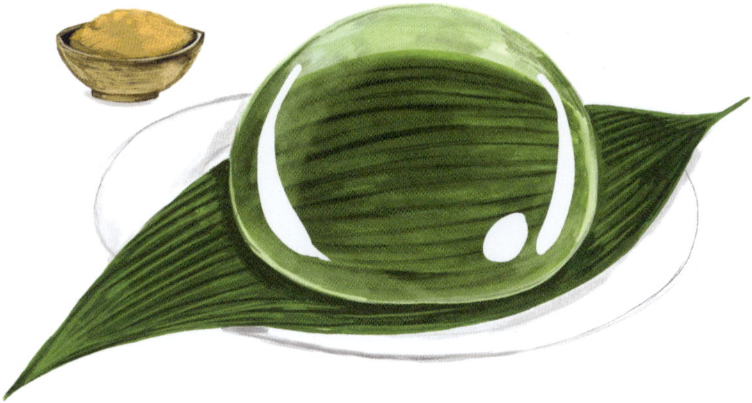

Raindrop Cake with Kinako

What you might recognize as the viral, trendy Raindrop Cake is known traditionally as *mizu shingen mochi,* literally "water confection" in Japanese. Made with little more than agar jelly and water set in a large spherical mold, it was invented in a traditional Japanese treat shop in Yamanashi Prefecture to celebrate the region's famously delicious water. But dessert lovers know that even delicious water still needs *a little* something-something. So this breathtaking orb is served with a sprinkling of kinako, a peanut-buttery roasted soybean powder, and lashings of mitsu, an old-fashioned black syrup made from unrefined muscovado sugar.

I know very well that this dessert is going to be hard to find because I have searched deep into blogs, videos, and social media pages for anyone making it in all the big US and Canadian cities I have visited in the last few years. I even set out on a long trip to visit a historic NYC market where I found that the food stall of a famous Raindrop Cake maker was no longer in existence. The farthest I've gotten in this quest to taste one of these supernatural balls of water is a promise from chef Darren Wong to make me a good one if I'm ever in LA. Darren, I promise here and now that I'll be holding you to it!

The Raindrop Cake is the only dessert in this book that I haven't tasted myself. I'm recommending it to you because sometimes it's fun to set out on a difficult quest for something unusual. Even though most experienced commenters declare that this dessert tastes of little more than water, that is hardly the point. Consider this an exquisite prize, what the avid birders call a *lifer*: the most elusive bird and greatest challenge on their list.

Apparently, even in *Japan* a Raindrop Cake is hard to find, available only at select confectioneries on special holidays. So while your worldwide quest unfolds, you might like to try something similar in spirit and composition to a Raindrop Cake: Anmitsu, a Japanese dish made with translucent agar cubes flavored with green tea or juice and garnished with sweet bean paste, rice flour dumplings, and fruit.

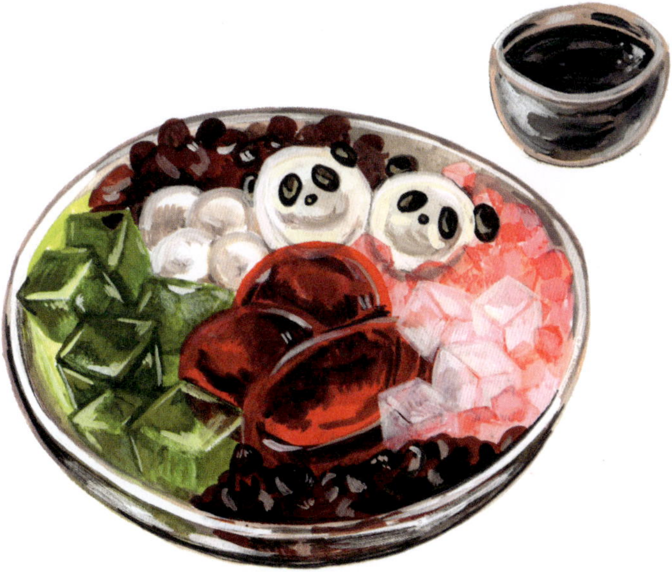

Anmitsu

This pretty bowl is ubiquitous on menus in Japan and should be considerably more available than Raindrop Cakes elsewhere in the world. Anmitsu is properly served with the same mitsu syrup, offered in a little pitcher to pour all over your colorful medley of angular platonic solids and pastes (and maybe some kawaii anime characters). Sometimes a dainty sphere of ice cream is tucked in too, melting around this pretty, texturally varied, and cooling treat.

Rhubarb Pudding

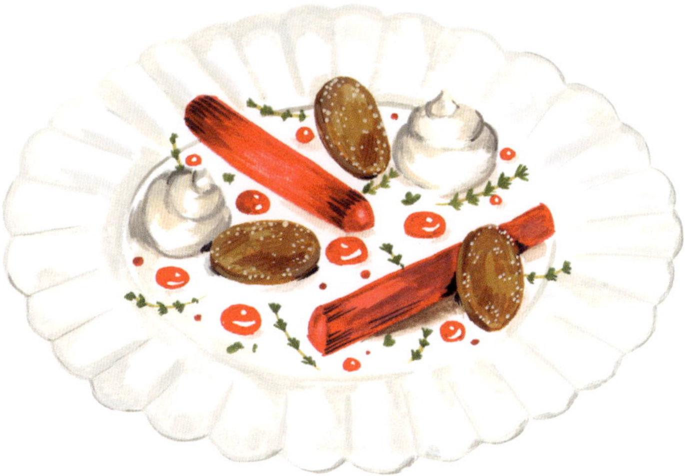

Deconstructed Rhubarb Pudding

The moment you enter the Museum of Icelandic Sorcery and Witchcraft, after a long drive from Reykjavík past desolate lava fields, when you are damp and chilled and hungry, you might be greeted by a surprising and heavenly smell: warm, buttery, cinnamon-garnished Rhubarb Pudding. What is this benevolent magic? Is it a traditional folk remedy? Viking medicine? It might be, but mostly the museum tearoom bakes this cake every afternoon because butter is so plentiful on an island full of grazing dairy animals. And the pie plant, as rhubarb is sometimes called, is one of the only things that grows in blustery, cold, rainy Iceland.

Rhubarb is the hardiest and the humblest of vegetables. With the leaves being poisonous and only the cooked stalk palatable, the only way to temper rhubarb's tannic, mouth-puckering astringency is to blanket it in butter, syrup, and cream. Its soft, melting texture also takes well to contrasting pastry, crisp accompaniments, and garnishes, so there are all sorts of rhubarb crumbles, cobblers, squares, pies, grunts, ice creams, and cakes—or, as the English call them all, *puddings*. In any of its guises, under the grayest sky, after the coldest winter, in a place where anything so tender as a strawberry would never dare to ripen, a Rhubarb Pudding casts a comforting spell.

Even if it's not raining where you are, there are many reasons to try rhubarb. Have you seen how the ruby spears of rhubarb can be sliced on an angle and tiled in a striking herringbone pattern on top of a cake? How pieces of rhubarb placed in an ombré color band can paint a spectrum of sunset colors from pale green to blush to the hottest, brightest pink? Wherever you find yourself—whether a cozy English-style café like Tea & Sympathy in New York, where they drown a rhubarb crumble (and all your troubles) in a deep bowl of warm custard, or a fancy restaurant where the Rhubarb Pudding might be meticulously arranged in a composition inspired by haute cuisine—order the Rhubarb Pudding. It is a charm and a balm for all of us weary, wind-chilled witches.

Royal Falooda

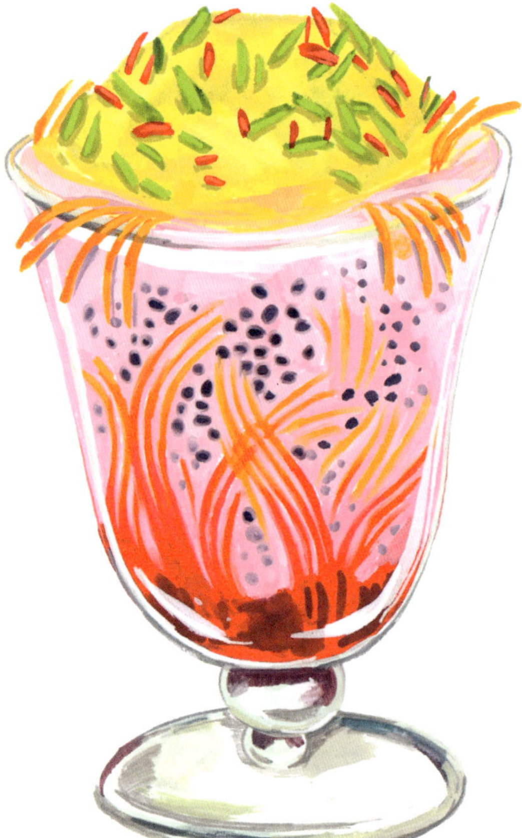

Royal Falooda

Is there yet another dessert you should taste with a spectrum of colors and a riot of textures all layered extravagantly in a tall, clear glass? Absolutely. Even when it comes in an opaque plastic cup from my local Indian snack café, Royal Falooda represents another incomparable experience in the dessert beverage / parfait / sundae cornucopia. A proper Royal Falooda is blooming with everything rose-flavored, hot pink, and sweet. It's dotted with black gelatinous seeds from the basil plant that look striking against sweetened milk and cream. It *also* contains vanilla or saffron ice cream, a scattering of pistachios or candied fruit, too much red syrup oozing over the rim of the glass, and we're not even done yet! These paradisiacal things are swimming in all directions with the signature element of a Royal Falooda: an immoderate helping of cold, unruly vermicelli noodles.

While such a refreshing noodle-based dessert may have been enjoyed in the Persian Empire since at least the 16th century, Royal Falooda is still a fashionable treat among South Asians, particularly in India, Pakistan, Bangladesh, and their diasporic communities around the world. And of course, it's hot outside, more often than ever, isn't it?

In its finest saffron- and rose-flavored incarnation, this icy dessert is fit to cool a prince on the hottest afternoon of the summer—or any citizen, like you, when it feels like your sandals are melting onto the pavement and you're craving a dose of vitamin pink. Look for a Royal Falooda to stir and slurp and spill all over from a street vendor or curry joint near you.

Soufflé Pancakes

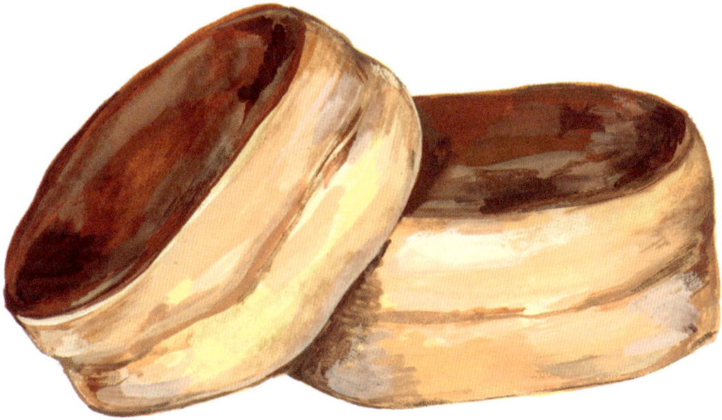

Soufflé Pancakes

Sweet pancakes in all their forms are beloved around the world. From Canadian hotcakes doused with maple syrup, to Moroccan semolina baghrir scented with honey and orange blossom, they are quick and easy to make (compared to an oven-baked cake) and a quintessential comfort food. Just stir up a simple eggy batter with leavening agents and sugar, and pour it into a buttered pan. Slather your plateful of speed-cakes with everything sweet and sticky and seasonal that you've got on hand, and enjoy a portal directly back to those mornings when you were allowed to stand on kitchen chairs and eat sweets for breakfast. Or when you drank strong mint tea with your mama, who generously piled lacy pancake after lacy pancake onto your sticky plate.

I can hardly justify focusing on only one pancake in this book, but for reasons of availability in different cities, urban fashion, and pure delight, I'm going to recommend that you find a dedicated Soufflé Pancake café or shop. There are more than a few in my own city—near the colleges and universities and especially in Chinatown and Little Korea—selling what are sometimes branded as Japanese Soufflé Pancakes. You'll know you have found them by their pudgy profile, pictured in the windows like stacked slabs of cumulus clouds.

Soufflé Pancakes have a texture that is like a cross between custard, cake, and spongy memory foam. Let me tell you just how much I would love to sleep in a warm, sumptuous bed of them! As with any soufflé, it takes quite a bit of technical skill and equipment to mold and steam these into a perfect state of loftiness, making them nearly as tall as they are wide. You may have to wait like I did, getting hungrier and hungrier, as long as *twenty-five minutes* for the pancakes to be custom made upon ordering. But when your hot, wobbly pancakes come to the table, they seem so much more than pancakes, even a little *alive*. You might forget how expensive they were too, because when was the last time someone made a soufflé for you and slathered it with matcha sauce or brown sugar boba pearls or chocolate and bananas or strawberries and cream? Be sure to devour them in a contented hurry before the wind blows all those lovely, airy pancakes right off your plate.

STICKY TOFFEE PUDDING

Sticky Toffee Pudding is a classic British ensemble of cake, sauce, and cream. This particular composition is so British, in fact, that Queen Elizabeth was said to have enjoyed it on cold days at her cottage in Balmoral, and (if you believe the gossip) it's Kate Middleton's favorite dessert. Isn't it fun to picture the pretty and polished Princess of Wales eating bite after oozing, scrumptious bite?

While the cake part of the dessert is almost homely—made with dates, cinnamon, ginger, and nutmeg—the secret to the appeal of Sticky Toffee Pudding is the way the sponge itself sits in a bath of buttery sauce, made with black sugars and molasses caramelized to the brink of ruin. The whole thing is almost boozy with intensity. Then this cakey soup is topped extravagantly with cream or, for the fanciest effect, with a sprinkling of sea salt and a dollop of contrastingly tart crème fraîche.

Sticky Toffee Pudding is also in the repertoire of another British (honorary) royal, the cookbook author, TV chef, and glamorous megastar Nigella Lawson. In one of her special holiday episodes, with Christmas ornaments dangling all around her kitchen, Lawson describes the classic, 1970s-era version of this dessert as a British tradition worth honoring. She admires all the recipe's various alchemies—melting dates in baking soda and browning sugars over a flame—and describes the sticky, viscous pudding sauce as having a "somber majesty." While she pours it thickly onto a cozy slab of cake in a shallow dish, Nigella flashes a look of total ravishment.

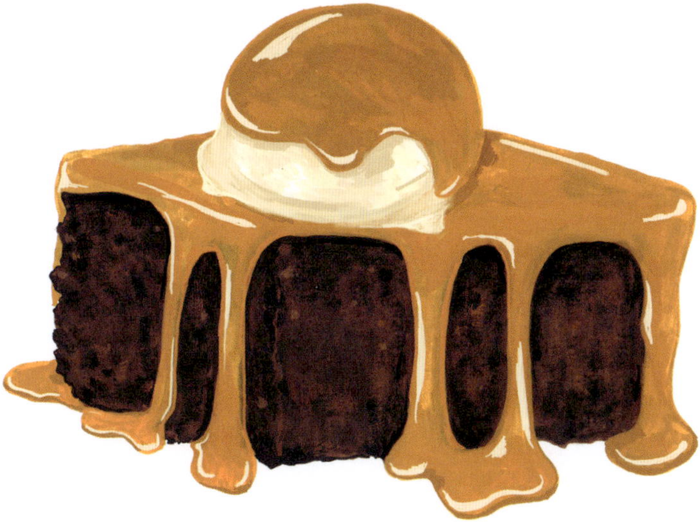

Sticky Toffee Pudding

Enjoy this dessert, properly warmed, the moment the first leaf falls from the trees. Source it from whichever English teahouse or bakery or restaurant you can find it in. After all, "it's not the time of year for restraint," Nigella says, "but when is it, really?"[9] When it comes to dessert, one should always obey the queen.

Strawberry Shortcake

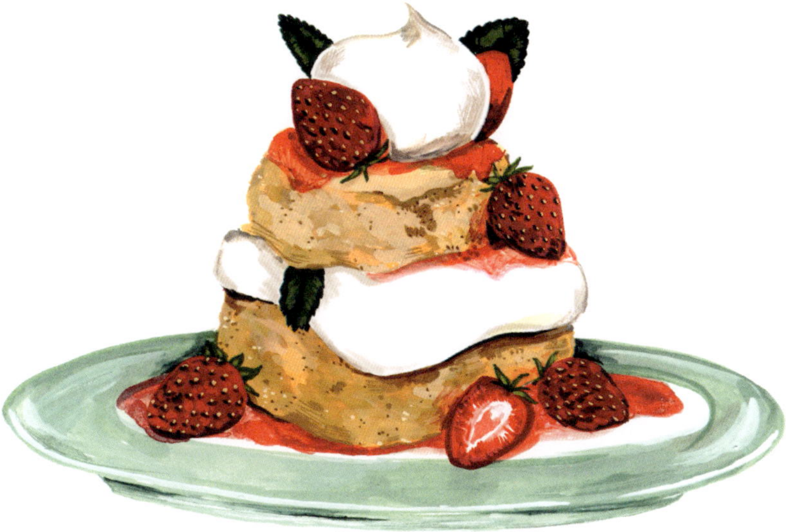

Strawberry Shortcake

In her beloved book *Braiding Sweetgrass*, Potawatomi author, scientist, and mother Robin Wall Kimmerer writes about collecting fragrant, ripe strawberries as a child behind her home. Her mother would use them to make a Strawberry Shortcake for her father. With fingers stained by sticky red juice, the young Kimmerer ate as many as she gathered. She recognized that the fields were full of treasures—including strawberries, raspberries, blackberries, hickory nuts, and wildflowers—that were free and beckoned to her. "In Potawatomi," she writes, "the strawberry is *ode min*, the heart berry,"[10] and it is the first thing harvested in the spring. To Kimmerer, the earth communicates profound truths through its forms. The heart-shaped strawberry reminds her, and should remind us all, of the loving gifts from nature. How should we respond to this great generosity? "Sometimes it feels like a silly question with a very simple answer: *eat them*," Kimmerer writes, and so we shall.

For much of the year in Canada, strawberries are only available in groaning plastic tubs that are shipped in from afar. In the winter, the berries themselves are pale and inflated, hollow, and tart as a lemon (with none of a lemon's charms). It is not until June, under what is sometimes called the *strawberry moon*, that the real, ruby-red strawberry is harvested around the country, cultivated in the sunshine on farms and sprouting all over from lengths of slender runners in the wild.

There are thousands of dessert recipes in which to enjoy them, and I wholly endorse testing and tasting every single delicious one of them. But in June, at the moment when strawberries are bright red through to their middles, choose the one perfect podium for their most complete adoration: Strawberry Shortcake.

You can easily assemble a Strawberry Shortcake at home or find one in a country bakery, teahouse, or restaurant attuned to seasonal ingredients. While there is a popular American version made with strawberries and cream between tidy layers of sponge cake, my favorite comes from English baking traditions. It features sliced and sugared strawberries stuffed loosely into a bed of warm, buttery scone. The fruit releases its crimson juice all over a velvety blanket of soft whipped cream. There is no better way to honor nature's sweetest gifts in spring, and nothing more delicious.

Taiyaki

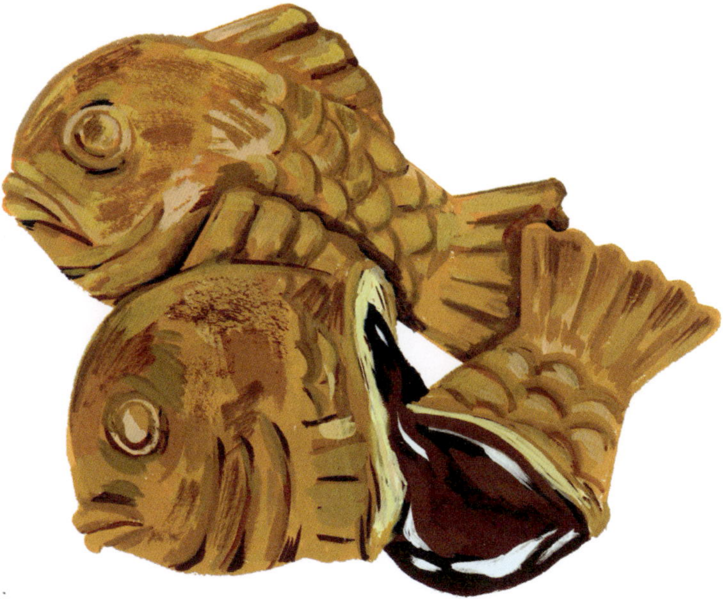

Taiyaki with Nutella Filling

You don't *have* to be enrolled in an endurance marathon of swimming lessons, suffering the cold water at a pool in Toronto in January, to enjoy a Taiyaki. But the one I had when I was hungry (and probably a little hypothermic) from backstroking all day was the best I have ever tasted.

I walked into my favorite Korean grocery store and made a beeline toward the rows of hot electric skillets shaped like giant goldfish. Filled on two sides with pools of waffle batter and dollops of firm yellow custard (or squidges of red bean paste), the waffles in progress were frying and steaming. They smelled so warm and sweet. I have never searched for coins and cash more urgently to pay for one $3 treat. Once it was tucked fresh from the griddle into a sleeve of parchment, I shark-attacked the smiling fish-shaped waffle nose first, while it was almost too hot.

The ingredients in that Taiyaki included wheat flour and sticky rice flour, which probably accounted for the uniquely chewy sweetness of the crisp waffle scales and fins. While I love a proper, homemade, egg-based custard, my favorite Taiyaki filling is actually made with industrialized custard powder. It is waxy, yellow, and by definition a very poor facsimile of the real thing. But definitions don't always rule desserts! I am smitten with this specific combination of textures. A Taiyaki's flavors are as reliably sweet and pleasing as modern chemistry allows. While I walked around the grocery store, without even a drop of the stiff filling oozing onto my shoes, I found myself trolling the aisles for a can (a box?) of the faux custard so I could try to make my own waffles at home.

Taiyaki is a street treat you can smell first (a strategic marketing strategy) when you are marching around the city in Korean, Japanese, and Chinese neighborhoods. I get mine at a grocery store, but there are dedicated shops on street corners or in food courts that you can identify by their perfume and by the sight of the large lucky carp silhouette. Keep an eye out! To avoid taxing your hungry, city-weary brain, the vendors will usually only ask you to decide among the most typical fillings: "custard," red bean paste, or a generously melting Nutella. Don't worry, any choice you make will be the right one. Your handheld waffle will be ready fast and piping hot. This is surely the easiest fish you will ever catch.

Tanghulu

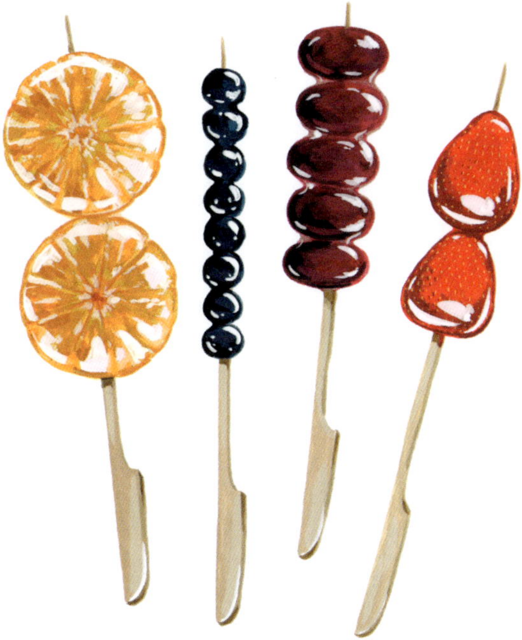

Tanghulu

The legend of this street treat from northern China begins more than a thousand years ago in the Song dynasty, when a concubine of the emperor became so sick that she lost her appetite. At that time, contrasting sweet and sour flavors were used to assist digestion and to balance the body's uneven energies. According to the story, when doctors fed her a prescription of tart red hawthorn berries boiled in sugar, she was miraculously cured.

The skewered jewels of glassy fruit we recognize today as Tanghulu are direct descendants of the hawthorn berry–inspired sweets popularized so long ago. Since then, Tanghulu artisans have experimented with crab apples, kumquats, and almost anything else you can think of to coat in hard candy and skewer on a stick. At festival stalls and in modern Japanese, Korean, and Chinese treat shops today, you can find everything from glittering green grapes, kiwi, pineapple, and strawberries to cucumbers, tomatoes, and even hard candy-coated *fried chicken*! What is really an old-fashioned and nostalgic treat has also become something of a sensation on TikTok. To the delight of millions of viewers, K-pop stars can be seen crunching through the thick cracking shells of their candy-coated strawberries in visceral ASMR videos, and influencers all over are stirring pots of thick, boiling sugar syrup and making their own Tanghulu.

While I'm disorientingly both attracted and repelled by all of this (Candy-coated chicken? Pretty models crunching on what sounds like shards of glass?), I notice that just writing about it all makes my mouth water. The first time I saw a display of spears of Tanghulu radiating out from a foam base at a shop in the trendy Harajuku neighborhood of Tokyo, it made me think of a Christmas tree in an ice storm. With every glittering branch so heavy with glaze, the whole startling display looked like it would clink and jingle and chime in the wind.

Shops sometimes warn patrons that both the candy shell and the skewers of Tanghulu can be sharp. I wondered whether a bite of this beautiful dessert would cut open my mouth! Since I was determined that the experiment must go on, I decided to accept the risk. I carefully bit through the delicate, crystalline glaze and into an extra-pliant, juicy red berry. I can confirm: Tanghulu is crunchy, juicy, surprising, and delightful. If not for the legend, the colors, the bold flavor combinations, and the viral trendiness, then try it for a tingly sense of danger. Talk about commanding one's attention! After licking the last strawberry juices and candy shards from the bamboo skewer left in my hands, I can report that, at least for me, this sensational dessert caused no injuries.

In her wonderful essay on Tanghulu, author Jess Eng writes about the magic of this bedazzlement, describing how a thin, glistening sugar shell "transforms ordinary fruit into *diamonds*."[11] I can hardly think of any other $5 experience that might supply such an encounter with pure brilliance.

TIRAMISU & BANANA PUDDING

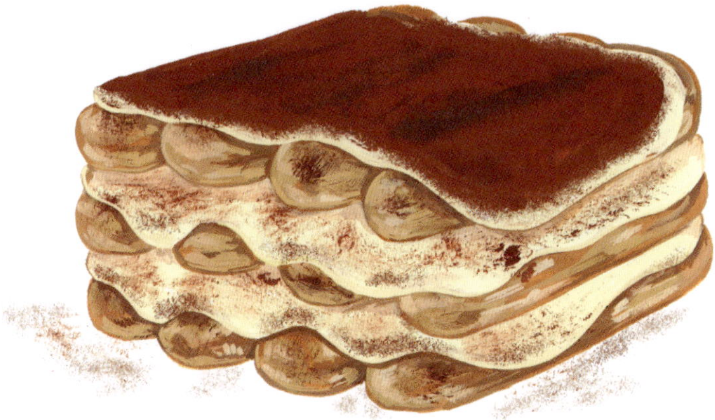

Tiramisu

The first memory I have of Tiramisu in my own Italian family is of eating large spoonfuls of it from deep Pyrex dishes at other people's houses. Occasionally, after a heavy restaurant dinner, we would order it for an equally heavy dessert. These Tiramisus were always homey recipes made with layers of mascarpone cream, eggy custard, and pumice-dry ladyfinger biscuits soaked in a syrup of strongly brewed espresso and marsala wine. It wouldn't be a Tiramisu unless the whole thing was dusted with a thin, velvety blanket of cocoa powder. I didn't really appreciate this boozy, adult dessert as a child. But today Tiramisu always reminds me of the Italian Canadian culture I grew up in, where a little coffee, a little alcohol, and even a daily ration of cookies were not only encouraged but actually considered *good for you.* This is some of the ancestral wisdom I have used to write this book and—gratefully—to live my life.

While my own mother was fonder of translating Italian expressions into English than she ever was of baking, she used to explain to us that *tira mi su* means, literally, "pick me up." The history of this dessert, whose signature flavors are coffee, sweet cheese, chocolate, and alcohol, is as swampy as its structure. Whether the caffeine perked up Venetian students before their exams or energized the weary after a visit to the brothel is unclear. But this confection is undisputably a modern classic, invented and popularized in the last fifty or sixty years. Now, Tiramisu has taken over the world.

Variations of the classic recipe feature Vietnamese coffee and condensed milk, or brandy, chocolate liqueur, coconut milk, or rum. The fanciest chefs deconstruct it into more elegant gastronomic assemblages, with cubes of cake, quenelles of mousse, and zabaglione piped in graceful swirls. And there are Tiramisu-flavored Mochi Donuts, cakes, Soufflé Pancakes, Canelés, and more.

Since I'm not much of a coffee lover, my favorite version of Tiramisu is actually a green one, made with a strong dose of matcha tea layered with cookies and cream. These are increasingly available where Asian sweets are sold, sometimes presented in

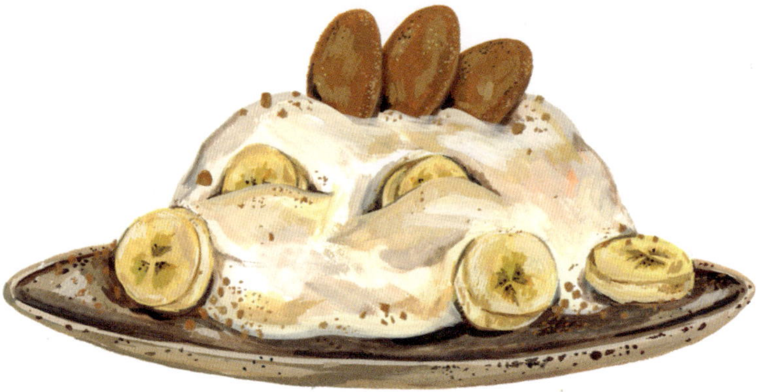

Banana Pudding

clear, dainty jars to show all the layers. I've even seen a cheeky, so-called *Tea-ramisu* made with reddish pandan-and-vanilla-flavored Thai iced tea, which I'm certain would complement a cozy red curry.

If you think you may need a slow-me-down instead of a pick-me-up but are still craving the sumptuousness of drenched biscuits drowned in custard, find yourself a good Banana Pudding. An iconic NYC version is layered with vanilla pudding, soaked cookies, and ripe banana slices, all mounded into a paper cup as high as gravity allows. This dessert, sometimes sprinkled with sweet coconut or thickened with sticky condensed milk (now I'm feeling really slow!) has been copied and perfected by dessert shops in cities everywhere. Like a classic Tiramisu, it's a formless treat that offers a soft blanket of comfort.

Tres Leches Cake

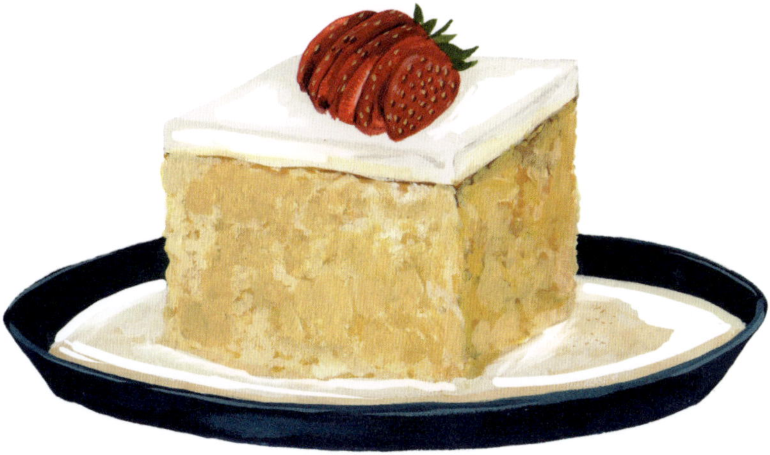

Tres Leches Cake

Tres Leches Cake is an enduring dessert for many good reasons. You are as likely to find one at a Latin American or Caribbean bakery as on a friend's kitchen table because it's such a beloved classic and simple to make at home. A light, airy vanilla sponge is set in a deep pool of *tres leches*, or "three milks": a silky sauce that typically includes whole milk for body, condensed milk for sticky sweetness, and evaporated milk for economy (at one time), plus nostalgia (here and now).

The history of Tres Leches Cake, like that of many desserts, is hard to draw out. Some consider this soaked cake a version of English trifle, which was developed in medieval times as a method of improving the palatability of stale bread. Others look to the popularity of another food preservation revolution from the more recent past. Between the World Wars, companies that sweetened and canned milk popularized the ingredients for cooking during periods of food shortage across Latin America. No matter the true origin, this comforting and luscious recipe became popular in the United States and abroad with Latin American immigration around the world.

Look for a neat square of Tres Leches Cake at a good Latin American restaurant or bakery. It may be sprinkled with a velvety layer of cinnamon and dotted with a sliced strawberry in the classic style. See if you can have it served in a deep, glorious pool of milky sauce with a spoon on the side (to drink it all up). This is ideally an afternoon dessert, eaten with a strong cup of coffee or with nothing at all, since your Tres Leches Cake is rich in egg yolks and already contains a glass of milk (or three).

I love the feeling of a drenched cake that just can't absorb another drop of milky abundance: its delicious *too-muchness*. It's hard not to think about the elemental longing that a taste of this generous, milky dessert might conjure. Tres Leches Cake is a sweet, uncomplicated embrace we remember from long ago—or maybe one we always wished we had.

Trompe l'Oeil Dessert & Entremet

In every reality baking show or viral cooking video, there is a moment when a sandal, a can of house paint, a tray of takeout chicken, or even what looks like the baker's own *head* is held up to a dramatically large knife and sliced. The pleasure comes as you realize that a thing you thought you understood is not at all as it seems.

In her *New York Times* article "Let Them Eat Fakes," Ligaya Mishan writes about the origins of the Trompe l'Oeil Dessert tradition, tracing it back to early examples of lavish fakery practiced in the kitchens of aristocrats and kings centuries ago. The richest people of all surely reveled in their power, devouring edible monuments, animals made of sponge cake, and detailed ornaments of sugar paste. "The cake is a cake," Mishan says. And the trick? Nothing less than "a beautiful lie."[12]

Even modern lovers of this trick delight in what Mishan calls a "jubilant shattering of illusions" over and over again. I suppose it is irresistible to see evidence that anything, anywhere could be miraculous, and that any ordinary thing could be an abundantly frosted pink and yellow *cake*.

As bewitching as this optical effect might be, we all know that slabs of sheet cake blanketed in heavy, sugary fondant are unlikely to taste good, and of course, that was never the point. But before you decide this isn't something you need to try, you should know there are versions of the Trompe l'Oeil Dessert

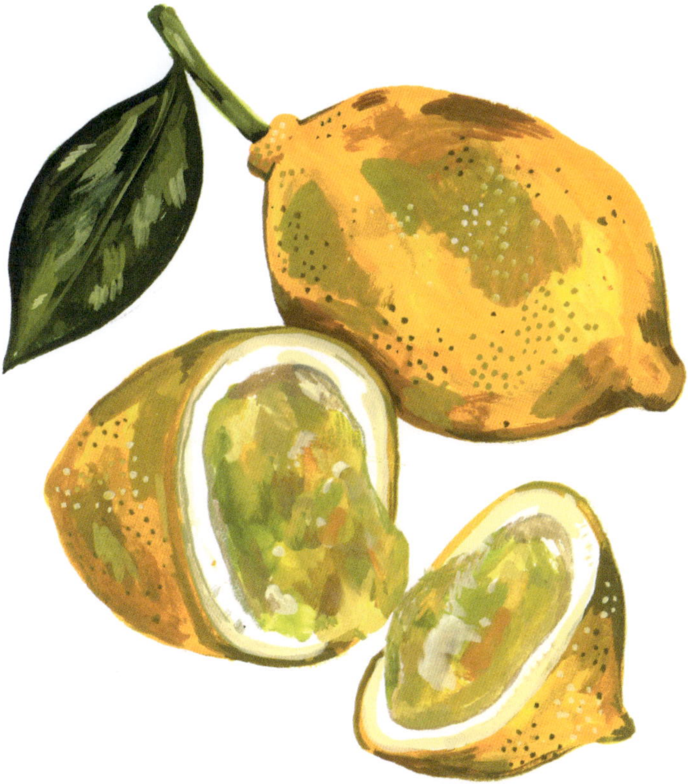

Trompe l'Oeil Citron by French Pâtissier Cédric Grolet

made by fashionable pastry chefs who care more about gastronomic experience than your average social media influencer does. These chef-artists tend to steer away from gimmicky, unappetizing subject matter, like handbags or shoes. Instead, they craft elaborate desserts that look like the delicious ingredients they are flavored with: a vanilla pod, a peach, or a bright yellow lemon with a fresh leaf still attached. If you can find a sensitively crafted example of a Trompe l'Oeil Dessert, note how the details have been rendered so intimately—even including, perhaps, a shiny drop of dew.

When you have a chance to visit a major pastry capital of the world—say Paris, Tokyo, Los Angeles, or London—it's going to take a little research to find the buzzy dessert of the moment. Prepare to put a dent in your wallet and to stand in line for the honor of tasting one.

When you slice into something like a Trompe l'Oeil citron by French pâtissier Cédric Grolet—made with a thin shell of fine white chocolate, poached lemon peel, fresh mint, and yuzu whipped ganache—you might discover it is not just *not a lemon*, but rather much *more* than a lemon. It is an ode to one.

I hope you can have an experience like this, but at the same time I hear your frustration. You want one of these impossible, edible artworks right now! I probably won't taste something made by Cédric Grolet again for many years, if ever again.

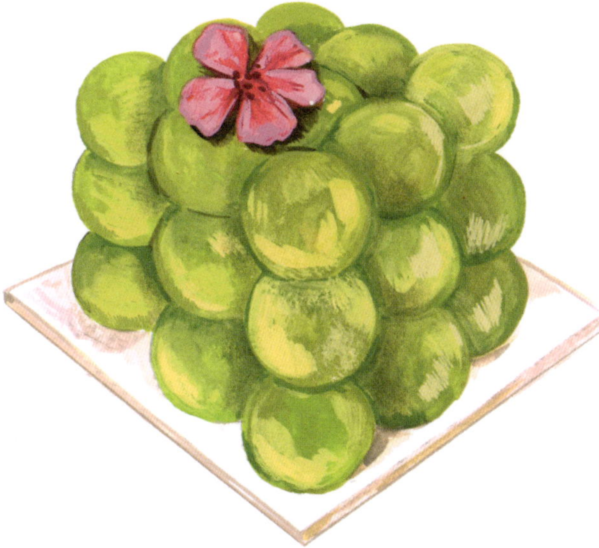

Citrus-and-Vanilla Entremet

While you and I both dream and wait, let's ease our appetites for a fancy dessert by acquiring a more accessible treat, available in any self-respecting dessert city at a more reasonable cost (and minus a flight to France).

An Entremet is technically any kind of fancy, layered dessert, usually including cake and mousse, and filled with an intense stripe of fruity jelly. A nice one might sit on a biscuity base and be decorated with fruit, flowers, and other ornaments, like macarons or wisps of chocolate. My favorites are the palm-size reveries intended to create a sequence of pleasing aesthetic experiences for a single person.

In Montreal, I came upon a stunning café that used the Entremet to show off all kinds of gastronomic invention and artistry. They offered a flame-orange, ovoid composition flavored with sea buckthorn berries and naturally maple-syrup-scented candy cap *mushrooms*. It was blazingly shiny and as aerodynamic as a race car. Another of their curious, minimalist offerings looked like a sphere of dark volcanic pumice garnished with a single yellow chrysanthemum petal. It was described as containing black garlic, white chocolate, sesame-honey crisp, a dacquoise biscuit, and a "carmine apple Bavarian cream." I'm not sure if "carmine" refers to the unusual African apple varietal or the bright red pigment derived from ground cochineal insects. I will live forever with the regret that I never tasted this adventurous dessert to find out.

Look for a classic Entremet wherever fancy pastries are sold. It might be cast in a groovy, 3D-printed geometric mold with a shiny mirror glaze or sprayed to look velvety and matte. Maybe you will even discover a gastronomic race car to ride in or a sphere of dessert ingenuity to orbit. In such a case, order both.

VANILLA CUSTARD TART & FRUIT CUSTARD TART

Oh, how many tarts I tasted for you! In my gritty city, it seems like there is a bakery on every street selling one kind or another. There are Hong Kong egg tarts (palm-size golden suns of sturdy, shiny filling in a thin crust pressed into tinfoil cups) and Portuguese pasteis de nata (little rustic cups of wavy, buttery pastry filled with cinnamon-scented custard, singed all over so, so enticingly). Wherever you are, I expect you will find a good version of a Vanilla Custard Tart. It might be what the French call a *flan pâtissier*, the South Africans call a *milk tart*, or the Americans—always nostalgic for grandmothers—an *old-fashioned custard pie*. There is also the ubiquitous Mexican flan, a crustless filling served on a plate in a pool of its own caramelized sauce. But I won't get into unbound custard here, since this entry is for the specific union of thick, eggy créme held in contrast within its most perfect companion, some crunchy pâtisserie grillée.

I am using fancy French terms here to give a little extra respect to this humble dessert, this perfect delight that is really just a crust filled with a quickly thickened soup of things that are probably already in your fridge. Germans might embed apples into a Vanilla Custard Tart, while others around the world have added a little flour, or a little cheese, or a splash of caramel. I love all the variations, but I will lose myself in the details of the simplest classic—cool, refreshing custard hovering in a state between liquid and solid, rising with my fork in a heap of slow flowing and gently folding wisps. All in a buttery scaffold, shattering and appeasing with every sumptuous bite.

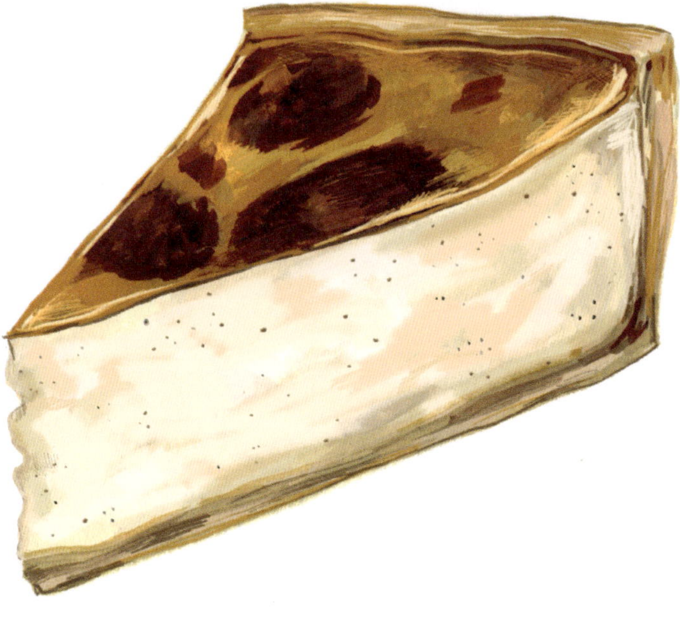

Vanilla Custard Tart

We sometimes need a reminder that despite its familiarity, vanilla is no ordinary thing. Rather, it's a precious and expensive flavoring, derived from the fruit of tropical orchids. As food critic Ligaya Mishan describes it, vanilla is "unruly" and "dark-sweet," "a summons of honeysuckle, sun-fat figs and red wine, of the dank sweetness of soil when the rain has soaked through it."[13] So when a dessert is made with pure extract like this—or even flecked with a constellation of tiny brown seeds scraped from the sticky, provocatively shaped pod—it is transformed into a form of rapture.

While a good Vanilla Custard Tart cannot be improved by much, I will concede one exception: a freshly made, seasonal Fruit Custard Tart. Raspberries, blackberries, strawberries, or any ripe tart fruit in season, strewn atop a biscuity crust full of custard like a pile of disorderly treasure, also makes a perfect thing. Let's praise every season with a custardy dish full of jewels like this one.

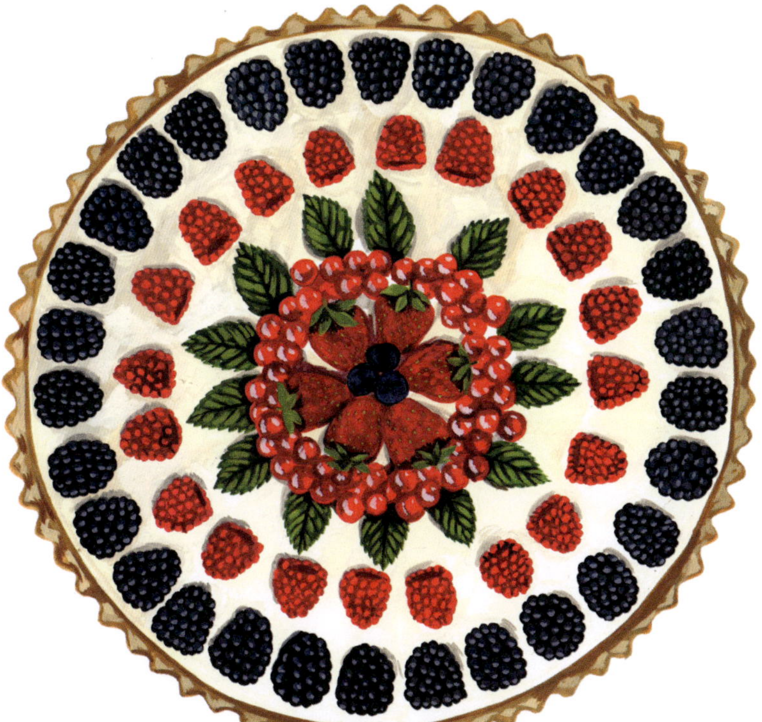

Mixed Berry Custard Tart

Wagashi

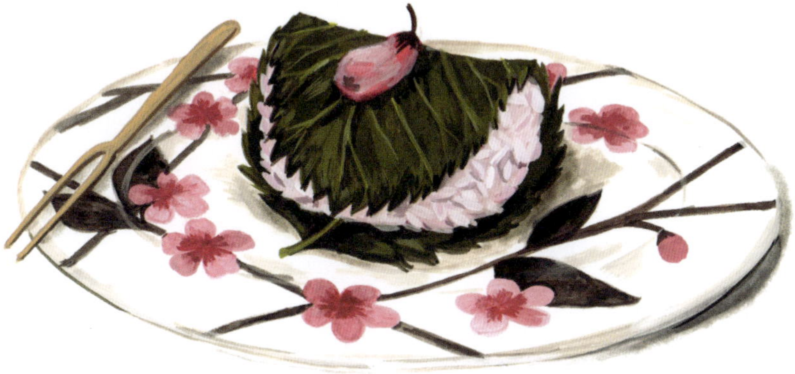

Spring Cherry Blossom Wagashi

"I didn't like tea as a child at first," the Japanese artist Mio Kamiya told the *Journal du Thé*. "That only changed when I learned that tea comes as a set, *with sweets*."[14]

Wagashi is the broad term for an encyclopedic variety of small, traditional sweets enjoyed with tea. They have been perfected by the most serious practitioners of confectionery craft in Japan for well over a thousand years. While a wide range of cakes, starchy jellies, and fried treats are available for any tea set, the term *Wagashi* most often refers to the raw sweets fashioned from mochi, or rice flour, and/or anko, a smooth, sweetened bean paste. In the hands of an expert confectioner, these malleable materials are kneaded and shaped into flowers, spirals, and half-moons, or they are pressed with dainty wooden tools into waves, swimming fish, or adorable bunnies. These small, edible sculptures are staged austerely on glazed plates, on blocks of wood, or among ornate packages. You can see them everywhere in Japan—from expensive department store food halls to small, family-run confectioneries to every neighborhood 7-Eleven convenience store.

Whether you are attracted more to the spare, geometric designs or to adorably pudgy Wagashi shaped like, say, the anime robot cat Doraemon, resist the urge to tear open the package and pop one into your mouth on your way out of a shop. You might find that the lovely, powdery dumpling is just too heavy and cloying to eat in one bite. Wagashi is a dense, sugary dessert that must be savored in small mouthfuls, with the counterbalancing effects of sips of a clear, fresh, or bitter tea. These contrasting sensory dimensions create the complete experience of Wagashi. Sweets and tea become one, like the light and the dark side of the moon.

If you are very lucky, you might find a teahouse where Wagashi are served with properly brewed teas or fresh matcha whisked into a creamy, green froth. There you might sit in silence, breathing in the aromas of roasting tea, flanked by a woman in a black dress with perfect posture and an elegant man with an infant asleep on his chest. While servers begin the graceful choreographies of tea service by ladling steaming water into

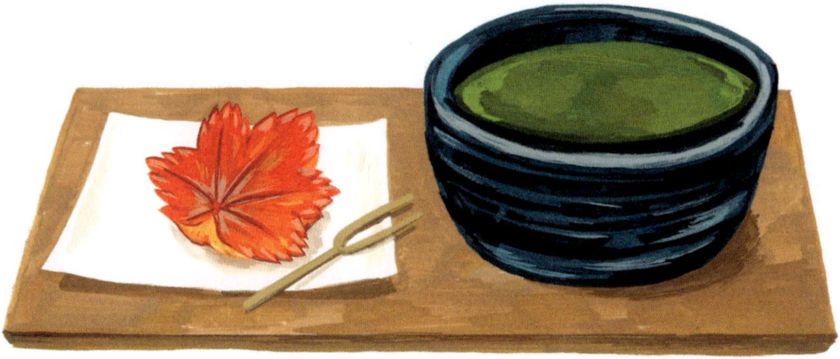

Autumn Leaf Wagashi and Matcha Set

your pot, you might have a long while to gaze at a curvy pine tree in the garden outside the window or at your handmade porcelain cup, sloping as if the clay were still in motion on a wheel. You will have enough time and silence to appreciate the luminosity of thin, translucent folds of white bean paste, tinted pale yellow, skin-soft, and folded into an edible, symmetrical bloom on your plate. The slowness and reverence of the tea ritual enable this appreciative gazing, touching, sniffing, nibbling, and sipping. A Wagashi is only one aesthetic element on this meditative stage, which, inspired by Zen Buddhist philosophy, invites you to an immersive, multisensory experience of the present moment. A particularly sweet one.

If you, like most of us, are outside of Japan and are craving Wagashi, you can find good examples of small tea desserts made with mochi, sweet bean, and other ingredients. Check for them at your favorite neighborhood ramen shop, at a Japanese-style convenience store, or in the bakery section of a Chinese or Korean supermarket. Many Wagashi—particularly baked, jellied, candied, or otherwise industrially preserved varieties—are shelf-stable and sometimes imported from Japan. Look out for seasonal, handmade treats like ichigo daifuku, which features a fresh red strawberry wrapped with bean paste in a small mochi pancake. Or savor a sakura mochi in springtime made with smooth mochi dough (or a bundle of sticky rice) filled with red bean paste and garnished with salt-pickled cherry blossoms. Celebrate the blossoming of the trees!

You could bring your 7-Eleven or supermarket Wagashi home to enjoy with tea in a precious cup. Or even better, bring one or two to the park for a picnic under a canopy of new green leaves. Clear a space for an impromptu ceremony in front of you, and in doing so, you'll also clear space in your mind. Remember Kakuzō Okakura, who in his famous treatise *The Book of Tea* says, "Let us dream of evanescence, and linger in the beautiful foolishness of things."[15] Brew and sip tea from a plastic bottle or your thermos, with much deliberateness and attention. Maybe your lower back will hurt from sitting on the ground. Maybe a guy will be conducting a business call too loudly beside you, or someone's wet dog will chase a sticky ball right over your legs. But while you nibble your sweets, feel the breeze lifting your hair, and breathe. Your tea set, no matter where you take it, creates a space for quiet pleasure in a noisy world.

War Cake

One of the many cakes I keep thinking about, among all the lavish desserts I tasted when writing this book, is the plainest brown Bundt cake I ever saw. In fact, it was only *half* a Bundt cake, hand-swaddled in plastic wrapping, in the dry goods section of a small grocery co-op in rural Nova Scotia. It was labeled "War Cake" and priced affordably, and the ingredients included little more than molasses, shortening, flour, spices, salt, and water, recalling a well-known recipe for an austere, long-lasting pantry cake developed during rationing in World War II.

It's a dessert paradox when cake, so often associated with happiness, abundance, and celebration, instead recalls a period of hunger and insecurity. Who would want to eat this? Then I remembered the American food writer M. F. K. Fisher's words in *How to Cook a Wolf*, published in 1942 during a period of wartime scarcities. She advised readers on thrifty ways to cook surprisingly elegant recipes "to live gracefully if we live at all"[16] even while the "wolf"—or starvation—was at the door. In chapters like "How to Be Cheerful Though Starving," she prompted her readers to remember that even in the midst of adversity, a creative cook can still find dignity and deliciousness.

For a few elders who shopped in the rural community supermarket, the humble War Cake that I saw must have contained a measure of comfort greatly exceeding the half cake's actual weight or flavor. Perhaps War Cake is made of *good* memories—of creativity and dignity under duress? From a period of fear

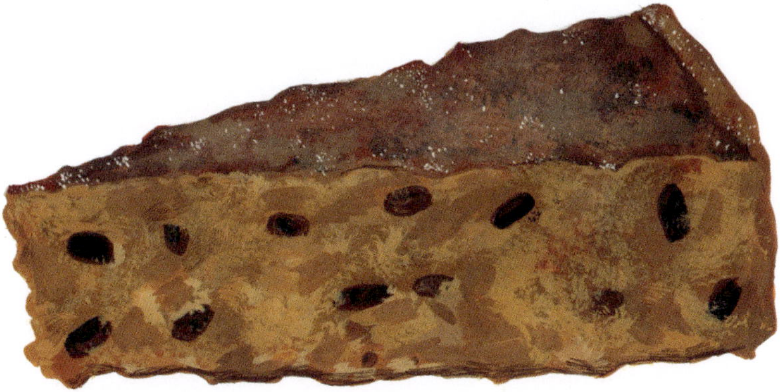

War Cake

and depletion, a low-cost slice of cake—no matter how butterless and plain—must have seemed like a dose of gladness.

It's cheering to know that War Cake is still for sale in the present, where calamities persist, both large and global and (as always) small and personal in scale too. A temporary refuge is necessary, wherever we can find it. We all need reminders that food is precious and that survival isn't just a matter of staying alive. It is a matter of *living*, wholly nourished.

Wild Blueberry Pie

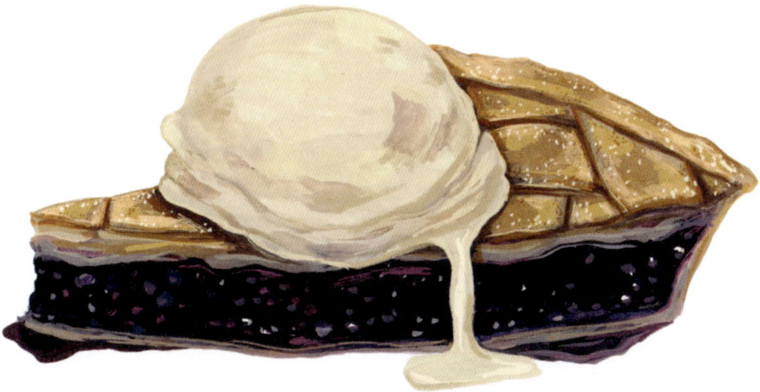

Wild Blueberry Pie

It has been so hard to decide which pie, or two or three, to include in this book, since I love any soft slurry of tart fruit wrapped in pastry. Don't we all? I hold on to how each classic embodies the changing seasons, landscapes, and weather, and look eagerly forward to them all. I'm thinking of a strawberry-rhubarb galette in spring, a spicy pumpkin pie in the fall, or a caramelized apple tart to get us through the winter. Pies fill us with nostalgia for pies of the past, and excitement for future pies to come. One might even say, with a bias toward sweetness, that the cycle of pie is one of the great cycles of our lives. With this much at stake, I narrowed things down to the great and fleeting pie of summer, one of the most consistently worshipped: Wild Blueberry Pie.

Granted, a slice of Wild Blueberry Pie is not easy to come by, especially in the city. The scarcity of this dessert is one of the factors that makes it so beloved and precious. You can be glad if yours doesn't demand a long, arduous hike up a mountain to pick blueberries in the beating sun. But be glad if it does too. Perhaps the steep hike, the heat, and the deerflies are behind you. You did it! And maybe you successfully made a pie yourself, or at least waited a long while for someone else to, folding in love along with the cold butter, handfuls of flour, sprinklings of sugar and lemon zest, and all that bloomy, indigo harvest. Be very thankful. Blueberries are northern jewels. I don't know if the whole boreal woodland is erupting with them, or if it is the miracle of the berries themselves that conjures the rest of the buzzy, mossy, coniferous forest. They ripen at the peak of summer in places where the season itself is a fleeting thing, never to be taken for granted.

The larger berries that we see in the supermarket all year long—cultivated commercially, plump with tart juice—make perfectly good pies. Go ahead and enjoy a blueberry pie made with commercial berries. Find one at a country bakery or your favorite pie shop where they don't craft them too sweet. Even better if they serve it warm, with a little cream.

But if you *do* find yourself among wild blueberries, and can resist eating them all immediately by the handful, you have the main ingredient of something special. At half the size of commercial berries, they seem to have twice the wine-like, deep, inky flavor—the distilled *essence of blue* concentrated into the bubbliest of packages. Even if it means an uncomfortable journey, hours of harvesting the tiniest of all fruit, and a tax paid in blood to the flies, it will be worth it. Even if the fresh berries, bursting in their densely jammy sauce, stain all your teeth and the teeth of your joyful, grinning dinner companions, a Wild Blueberry Pie is a kind of paradise. It's as wild and beloved as the northern summer itself.

ZOOLBIA
&
GAZ

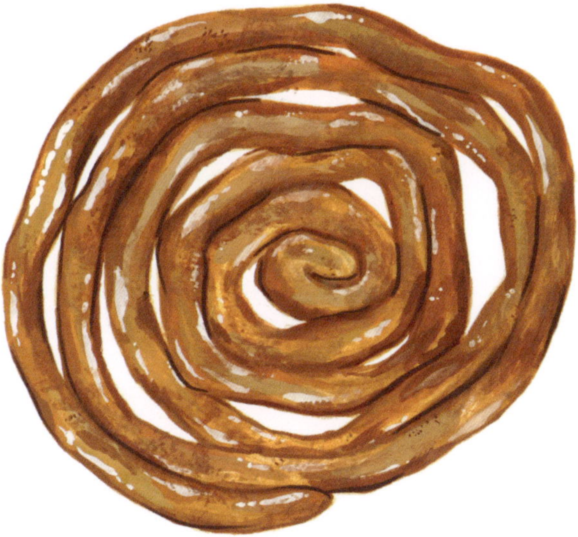

Zoolbia

Among the Persian sweets I can never resist is the shiny, spiraling Zoolbia. This edible ornament is fashioned from looping swirls of fermented yogurt batter, squeezed from a bottle into boiling oil. It is crisp, deliciously oily, and glowy as a rope of molten glass. When I see this delicate, saffron-colored fritter floating in a pool of shiny rose and honey syrup, it makes me wonder how many I could eat before I might involuntarily whirl up into the heavens. Could this centuries-old, elegant Middle Eastern dessert have been the original inspiration for the deep-fried funnel cake of American carnivals?

Another of my favorite Iranian sweets is Gaz, a marshmallowy nougat made with sugar and egg whites, sometimes called *Persian nougat*. It's often flavored with rosewater and studded with pistachios, almonds, dried fruit, and flower petals. I've seen Gaz in a wide range of forms and colors, including soft lumps dusted with icing sugar; chewy, tidy cubes; and cross sections of rolled candy that show off all their pretty ingredients in contrasting colors. This is the most opulent food. Your only problem will be which one to choose.

The way to find these sweets is to hunt for an austerely decorated Persian sweet shop with a case full of gorgeous enticements under a glittering chandelier. You can get your Zoolbia or Gaz to go, along with some powdery chickpea shortbread (which melts in the mouth) and snappy Persian pistachio brittle. But unless you have a Nowruz (Persian New Year) party to get to, stay right where you are and order your treats from a menu, along with some hot spiced cardamom tea. My bet is that your tea will come in a gilded glass, and your dessert on an ornamental tray made of silver. The entire ambience of the experience lends a little grace to the fact that you are licking syrup from your fingers, nibbling the pistachios that fell into your lap, swooning from the saffron, and fiddling a crisp little rose petal out from between your teeth. I promise you will feel fancy and happy nonetheless.

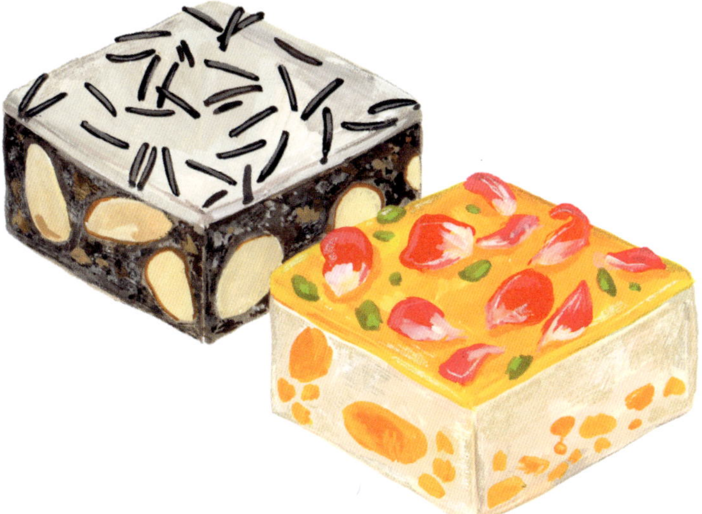

Gaz with Cookies and Cream, and with Apricots and Pomegranate Seeds

THE DESSERT CLUB

LIFE LIST

Use this handy list to keep track of all the desserts from this book you taste. See what you can find and experience in your own city, and in places you visit around the world.

You can also personalize the Dessert Club Life List by adding some of your own notable dessert experiences.

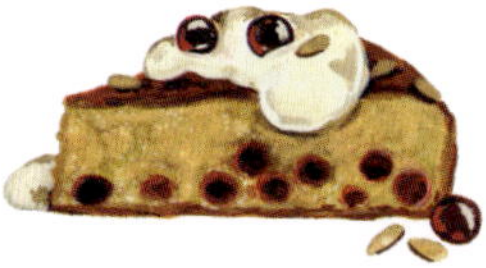

CAKES

☐ ALMOND CAKE

location: ....

date: ....

notes & rating: ....

☐ BISCOFF CHEESECAKE

location: ....

date: ....

notes & rating: ....

☐ CREPE CAKE

location: ....

date: ....

notes & rating: ....

☐ LAMINGTON

location: ....

date: ....

notes & rating: ....

☐ LAVA CAKE

location: ....

date: ....

notes & rating: ....

☐ MEDOVIK

location: ....

date: ....

notes & rating: ....

☐ PISTACHIO CAKE

location: ....

date: ....

notes & rating: ....

☐ RAINBOW CAKE

location: ....

date: ....

notes & rating: ....

☐ TRES LECHES CAKE

location: ....

date: ....

notes & rating: ....

☐ WAR CAKE

location: ....

date: ....

notes & rating: ....

☐ ______________________________

location: ....

date: ....

notes & rating: ....

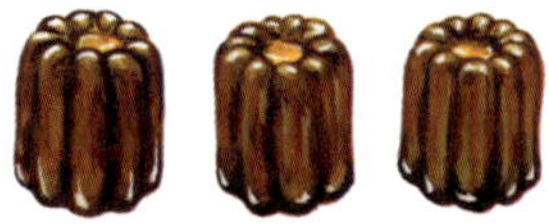

EUROPEAN CLASSICS

☐ CANELÉ

location: ....

date: ....

notes & rating: ....

☐ CANNOLI

location: ....

date: ....

notes & rating: ....

☐ CREAM PUFF

location: ....

date: ....

notes & rating: ....

☐ ÉCLAIR

location: ....

date: ....

notes & rating: ....

☐ LEMON LAVENDER SHORTBREAD

location: ....

date: ....

notes & rating: ....

☐ MILLE-FEUILLES

location: ....

date: ....

notes & rating: ....

☐ TIRAMISU

location: ....

date: ....

notes & rating: ....

☐ VANILLA CUSTARD TART

location: ....

date: ....

notes & rating: ....

☐ ____________________

location: ....

date: ....

notes & rating: ....

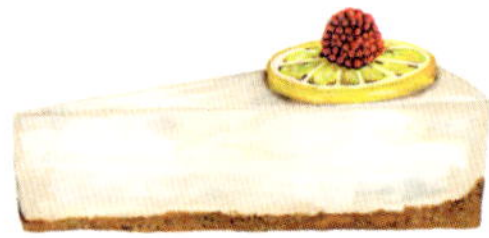

SUPERFOOD

☐ **FAT BOMB**

location: ....

date: ....

notes & rating: ....

☐ **PLANT-BASED CHEESECAKE**

location: ....

date: ....

notes & rating: ....

☐ ______________________________

location: ....

date: ....

notes & rating: ....

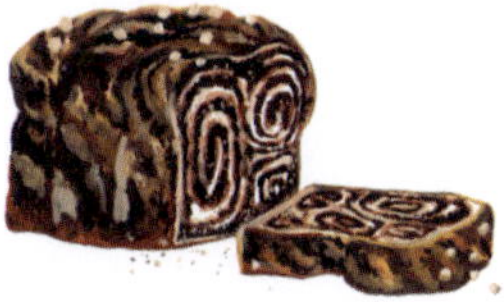

COMFORT

☐ BABKA

location: ....

date: ....

notes & rating: ....

☐ BANANA PUDDING

location: ....

date: ....

notes & rating: ....

☐ RHUBARB PUDDING

location: ....

date: ....

notes & rating: ....

☐ STICKY TOFFEE PUDDING

location: ....

date: ....

notes & rating: ....

☐ ______________________________

location: ....

date: ....

notes & rating: ....

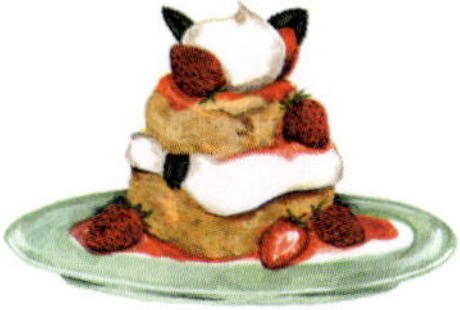

SEASONAL

☐ **FRUIT CUSTARD TART**

location: ....

date: ....

notes & rating: ....

☐ **MAPLE SYRUP PIE**

location: ....

date: ....

notes & rating: ....

☐ **MOONCAKE**

location: ....

date: ....

notes & rating: ....

☐ **STRAWBERRY SHORTCAKE**

location: ....

date: ....

notes & rating: ....

☐ **WAGASHI**

location: ....

date: ....

notes & rating: ....

☐ **WILD BLUEBERRY PIE**

location: ....

date: ....

notes & rating: ....

☐ ____

location: ....

date: ....

notes & rating: ....

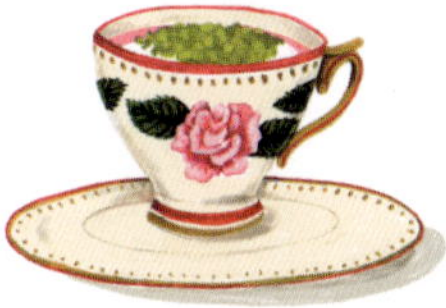

DRINKABLE DESSERT

☐ BUBBLE TEA (CONTEMPORARY)

location: ....

date: ....

notes & rating: ....

☐ BUBBLE TEA (TRADITIONAL)

location: ....

date: ....

notes & rating: ....

☐ CHOCOLATE SHOT

location: ....

date: ....

notes & rating: ....

☐ **KASHMIRI CHAI**

location: ....

date: ....

notes & rating: ....

☐ ____

location: ....

date: ....

notes & rating: ....

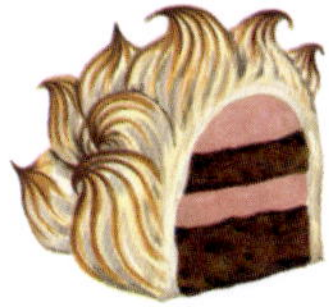

ICY

☐ **BAKED ALASKA**

location: ....

date: ....

notes & rating: ....

☐ **BINGSU**

location: ....

date: ....

notes & rating: ....

☐ **BOOZA**

location: ....

date: ....

notes & rating: ....

☐ **CHARCOAL ICE CREAM**

location: ....

date: ....

notes & rating: ....

☐ **KAKIGORI**

location: ....

date: ....

notes & rating: ....

☐ ____

location: ....

date: ....

notes & rating: ....

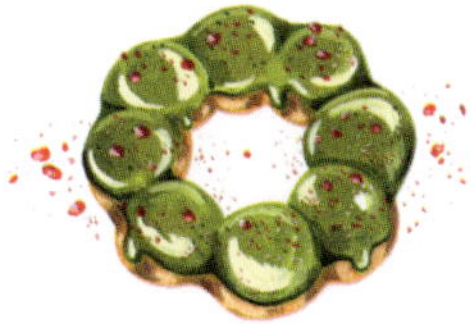

FRIED

☐ BACON DONUT

location: ....

date: ....

notes & rating: ....

☐ GULAB JAMUN

location: ....

date: ....

notes & rating: ....

☐ MOCHI DONUTS

location: ....

date: ....

notes & rating: ....

☐ TAIYAKI

location: ....

date: ....

notes & rating: ....

☐ ZOOLBIA

location: ....

date: ....

notes & rating: ....

☐ ____

location: ....

date: ....

notes & rating: ....

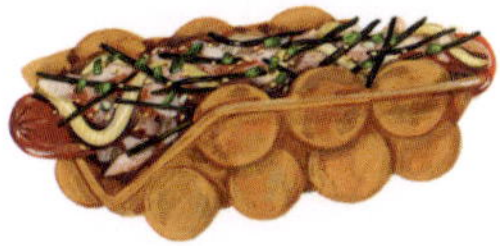

FUN

☐ BUBBLE WAFFLE HOTDOG

location: ....

date: ....

notes & rating: ....

☐ CUPCAKE WITH BUTTERCREAM

location: ....

date: ....

notes & rating: ....

☐ FRUIT SANDO

location: ....

date: ....

notes & rating: ....

☐ ICE CREAM SANDWICH

location: ....

date: ....

notes & rating: ....

☐ **PINEAPPLE CHAMOYADA**

location: ....

date: ....

notes & rating: ....

☐ **SOUFFLÉ PANCAKES**

location: ....

date: ....

notes & rating: ....

☐ **TANGHULU**

location: ....

date: ....

notes & rating: ....

☐ ____

location: ....

date: ....

notes & rating: ....

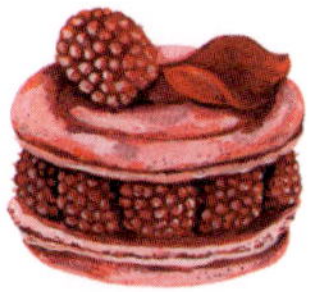

ELEGANT

☐ **ANMITSU**

location: ....

date: ....

notes & rating: ....

☐ **ENTREMET**

location: ....

date: ....

notes & rating: ....

☐ **GAZ**

location: ....

date: ....

notes & rating: ....

☐ **ISPAHAN**

location: ....

date: ....

notes & rating: ....

☐ KUNAFA

location: ....

date: ....

notes & rating: ....

☐ MAHALABIYEH

location: ....

date: ....

notes & rating: ....

☐ PAVLOVA

location: ....

date: ....

notes & rating: ....

☐ SWEET CORN, TAPIOCA, AND COCONUT PUDDING

location: ....

date: ....

notes & rating: ....

☐ ____________________

location: ....

date: ....

notes & rating: ....

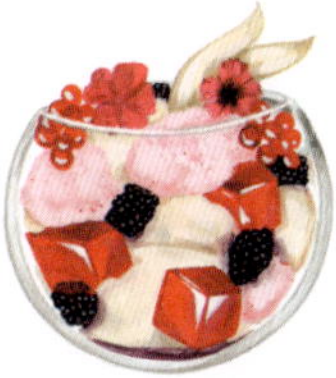

EXTRAVAGANT

☐ COCONUT JELLIES

location: ....

date: ....

notes & rating: ....

☐ FLOWER PARFAIT

location: ....

date: ....

notes & rating: ....

☐ HALO-HALO

location: ....

date: ....

notes & rating: ....

☐ MANGO POMELO SAGO

location: ....

date: ....

notes & rating: ....

☐ MATCHA PARFAIT

location: ....

date: ....

notes & rating: ....

☐ MONT BLANC

location: ....

date: ....

notes & rating: ....

☐ ROYAL FALOODA

location: ....

date: ....

notes & rating: ....

☐ ______________________________

location: ....

date: ....

notes & rating: ....

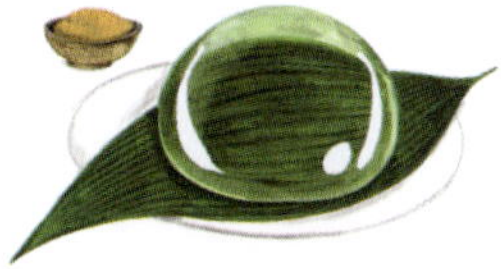

RARE

☐ RAINDROP CAKE

location: ....

date: ....

notes & rating: ....

☐ TROMPE L'OEIL DESSERT

location: ....

date: ....

notes & rating: ....

☐ ____________________

location: ....

date: ....

notes & rating: ....

ACKNOWLEDGMENTS

First, thank you to the bees for honey, the chickens for eggs, the trees for mangos and maple sap, the cows for milk and cream, and the sun for giving all plants and animals what we need to make sweetness. Thank you to the farmers and harvesters and especially the bakers, chefs, servers of tea, and pipers of choux and buttercream flowers—your work is a gift and an art of the highest order.

Thank you to my family and friends, especially Shannon for smoky maple syrup, Glicelle for Halo-Halo, Olivia for the million-layer honey cake, Abby for Baked Alaska, and my mother-in-law, Anne, for birthday cakes and Wild Blueberry Pies. Thank you to Vesna and Nikolas, Zuzana and Mike, Kelly and Terence, and your brilliant families for love, food, and gatherings beyond counting. You are a cornucopia!

Thank you to the young critics and my friends Vuk, Anya, and Ella Jane for reviewing freakshakes with me for *Illustoria* magazine.

Thank you to Anna Comfort O'Keeffe, Harriet Alida Lye, Leslie Ting, Sameer Farooq, Jasmine Oore, Mat Karas, Kyo Maclear, and Elizabeth Haidle for friendship, inspiration, tea drinking, library writing, fancy restaurant visiting, cold swimming, and encouragment of my writing.

Love and gratitude to my mom (lover of Mango Pomelo Sago), my dad (for whom the cookie drawer was invented), and Zia Dora (for sharing the blackest tea with me, at any time of day or night).

Tremendous appreciation to everyone at Chronicle Books, especially my caring editors, Mirabelle Korn and Karah Bengs. Your insights and encouragement throughout this process have been as dear to me as matcha. And that is very dear! Thank you also to designers Kayla Ferriera and Zoë Carr; copyeditor Judith Riotto; Erin Thacker and Gabriel Martinez in production; and managing editor Michele Posner.

I am infinitely grateful for the wisdom, enthusiasm, and trust of Jackie Kaiser and her colleagues at Westwood Creative Artists, including Meg Wheeler and Bridgette Kam.

Thank you to my dear friend and illustrator Kelsey Oseid for expert conjuring of coconut flakes, chocolate ooze, and syrupy shine. You've made each dessert vibrate with life. I'm so thankful for your sympathetic brain, your work, and your company. I promise one day to bake a hearty, invincible War Cake just for you.

Thank you, Amish, for supporting all my obsessions with an open mind and a generous hand, and for all the chocolate and Thai Coconut Jellies delivered by bicycle. Let's eat everything in this book together, all over again.

Finally, this book is dedicated to Felix, my all-day-baking, chocolate-mastering, buttercream-piping, kitchen-demolishing, dessert-loving teenager. Thank you for the inspiration, the viral dessert advice, and for joining me on so many tasting adventures. I'm proud of you every day, Felix. I love you more than cake.

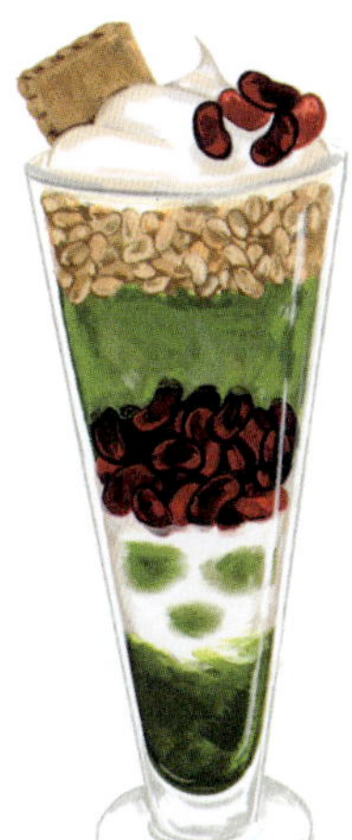

ENDNOTES

1 Nigel Slater, *A Thousand Feasts* (Fourth Estate, 2024), 3.

2 "A Day at a 143 Year-Old Restaurant with NYC's Most Iconic Desserts," *On the Line*, season 1, episode 4, *Bon Appétit*, 2022.

3 Sarah Ubertaccio, "The Story Behind Pasta Grannies: An Interview with Vicki Bennison," q.b. Cucina (online), January 20, 2023.

4 Elyse Inamine, "A Fruit Sando Is a Dessert Sandwich Filled with Joy and Whipped Cream," *Bon Appétit* (online), July 19, 2018.

5 Sam Dean, "Yotam Ottolenghi and the Authors of 'The Gaza Kitchen' Discuss Food, Conflict, Culture," *Bon Appétit* (online), March 27, 2013.

6 Alan Davidson, *Penguin Companion to Food* (Penguin UK, 2002), 605. Emphasis added.

7 Nicola Humble, *Cake: A Global History* (Reaktion Books, 2010), 54–55.

8 Erik Piepenburg, "What Is 'Queer Food'? A Conference Explores (and Tastes) Some Answers," *New York Times*, May 2, 2024.

9 "Sticky Toffee Pudding," *Nigella: At My Table*, BBC Two (online), 2017, YouTube.

10 Robin Wall Kimmerer, *Braiding Sweetgrass: Indigenous Wisdom, Scientific Knowledge, and the Teachings of Plants* (Milkweed Editions, 2013), 22.

11 Jess Eng, "Tanghulified," *Cake Zine: Candy Land 5* (2024), 23–24.

12 Ligaya Mishan, "Let Them Eat Fakes," *New York Times*, August 11, 2021.

13 Ligaya Mishan, "How Did Vanilla Become a Byword for Blandness?" *New York Times Style Magazine*, September 8, 2023.

14 "Mio's Contemporary Chinoiserie: Interview with Mio Kamiya," *Journal du Thé* (Poetic Pastel Press, 2018), 53.

15 Kakuzō Okakura, *The Book of Tea* (B. P. Putnam's Sons, 1906; repr., Stone Bridge Press, 2006), 16.

16 M. F. K. Fisher, *How to Cook a Wolf* (World Publishing, 1942; repr., First North Point Press, 1988), 7.